MORE THAN
A
GAME

MORE THAN

A GAME ⚘ ⚘ ⚘

Compiled by *A. LAWRANCE HOLMES*

MEYER BERGER • JIMMY BRESLIN • HEYWOOD BROUN • BARNABY CONRAD
BOB CONSIDINE • BILL CORUM • ARTHUR DALEY • JAMES P. DAWSON • ARTHUR
CONAN DOYLE • PAUL GALLICO • RING LARDNER • LEONARD LEWIN
A. J. LIEBLING • JOHN LOVESEY • JAMES MURRAY • DAN PARKER
QUENTIN REYNOLDS • GRANTLAND RICE • CARL T. ROWAN • DAMON RUNYON
WILLIAM SAROYAN • RED SMITH • AL STUMP • JOHN R. TUNIS • H. C. WITWER

Introduction by **PAUL GALLICO**

THE MACMILLAN COMPANY, *NEW YORK*

COLLIER-MACMILLAN LIMITED, *LONDON*

ACKNOWLEDGMENTS

Grateful acknowledgment is made to the authors, publishers and others listed below for permission to use the following stories:

"Undertaker Song," by Damon Runyon, which appeared in Collier's, copyright 1934 by Collier's, copyright 1962 by Damon Runyon Jr. Reprinted by permission of Damon Runyon Jr.

"Peanut Vendor," by Quentin Reynolds, which appeared in Collier's, copyright 1935 by Quentin Reynolds. Reprinted by permission of the estate of Quentin Reynolds.

"The Greatest Man," by Red Smith, which appeared in the New York Herald Tribune, copyright 1965 by the New York Herald Tribune and Publishers' Newspaper Syndicate. Reprinted by permission of the author.

"Is it Only a Game?" by William Saroyan, which appeared in Sports Illustrated, copyright 1956 by Time Inc. Reprinted by permission of author.

"Larsen Pitches First Series No-Hitter," by Dan Parker, which appeared in the New York Mirror, copyright 1956 by The Hearst Corporation. Reprinted by permission of The Hearst Corporation.

Paret Under Knife," by Leonard Lewin, which appeared in the New York Mirror, copyright 1962 by The Hearst Corporation. Reprinted by permission of The Hearst Corporation.

"Walcott-Charles Title Fight," by James P. Dawson, which appeared in The New York Times, copyright © 1951 by The New York Times Co. Reprinted by permission of The New York Times.

"Game Called," by Grantland Rice, from The North American Newspaper Alliance, copyright 1948 by the N.A.N.A. Reprinted by permission of The N.A.N.A.

"They'll Remember This One," by Bill Corum, which appeared in the New York Journal-American, January 2, 1934, copyright 1934 the New York Journal-American. Reprinted by permission of the New York Journal American.

"First World Series," from The American Way in Sport, by John R. Tunis, published by Duell, Sloan & Pearce, Inc., copyright 1958 by John R. Tunis. Reprinted by permission of Duell, Sloan & Pearce, Inc.

"Snead Loses 1939 Open," from Education of a Golfer, by Al Stump and Sam Snead, published by Simon & Schuster, Inc., and Cassell & Co., Ltd., copyright © 1962 by Sam Snead and Al Stump. Reprinted by permission of Simon & Shuster, Inc., and Laurence Pollinger Ltd.

INTRODUCTION

There are two factors that combine to make the unforgettable sports story: the event itself, or the character or characters involved and the witness thereto, the sportswriter, who reacts to what he sees and, filled with the excitement and the still reverberating echoes of the class of teams or individuals, sets his typewriter to churning. He is burning to let his readers share his experience, to make them see it, hear and feel it as he has, in short, to tell them the story of a marvelous happening.

The sportswriter's task is unlike any other, for when he takes a seat in the press box or ringside, he never knows what he is going to see. He can prepare neither his adjectives nor his state of mind. Something unforeseen and unpredictable is about to take place and he must attune himself to be the eyes and ears and the interpreter of the event for those who could not be there.

Daily, the sportswriter is confronted with what at the beginning of an afternoon is an unfinished play. The ingredients of a struggle and suspense have been brought together, but their outcome and attendant incidents are in the laps of the gods. The game or the clash may turn out to be a listless, thundering bore, with the spectators booing or whistling in discontent (itself a story), or it may blaze up into such a fury of competitive emotion that the fans leave shaken and drained. Injury and even death can turn what is in essence a mock drama into genuine tragedy.

One might think that modern broadcasting, radio and television, would usurp much of the sportswriter's province. You sit in your home; you see it take place; what need have you of a third party to tell you what has happened? Yet this is not so. The actual contest itself—football or baseball game, prize fight, golf or tennis match, is far from the whole story. You have seen only a part of it, the climax. The sportswriter must still produce the introduction to the conflict, the situation, the personalities, the stakes and, when it is over, the conclusions. Not even the ubiquitous and frequently too noisy commentator, whose voice accompanies the telepictures, can produce the whole into something rounded and satisfying. And, of course, not everyone can see it on television either, or hear it on the radio. The teller of sports stories will always be in demand.

Most of this collection of unforgettable tales from the realm of sport pre-date the recording mechanical eye, and are immortalized through the emotions of trained writers who saw what took place and were able to put it into words. Not all deal with collision on the field, but concern the often and even more fascinating side to games and gamesmanship, the characters of the players.

Here the sportswriter fulfills a special and unique function. He is closer to the performer than any spectator can hope to get. Often he sees him daily at practice or in his home, or is made his confidant. He has all the materials at his fingertips to weave into a coherent and fascinating narrative. If deeds performed by athletic prodigies are exciting, how much more stimulating it can be to learn what kind of people these were and what the distinguishing traits that enabled them to scale the heights.

The names in the table of contents read like a roster of my friends and colleagues from days gone by, when I worked side by side with Bill Corum, Grantland Rice, John Tunis, Dan Parker, Jim Dawson, Quent Reynolds, Bob Considine, Arthur Daley and Damon Runyon. They were all not only experts and keen observers, but master story-tellers as well, human beings who reacted emotionally to what they saw. They were never blasé; they always brought with them into the stadium freshness and the capacity to be stirred. They were ever alert for the unusual, the dramatic, the near-miraculous, in other words—the story. Many of them had the ability to see beyond what was transpiring to what lay behind it and expose the human strengths and weaknesses that went to make up the outcome of the battle.

This was a wonderful fraternity to which to belong and we lived on a constant peak of excitement. We were rivals and yet extraordinarily close friends, for each had his own style and approach to a story. Grantland Rice and I often traveled together sharing a stateroom, or sometimes it would be Considine or Runyon. But when they unlimbered their typewriters in the press box there was no point in trying to outwrite them, for they were all individualists and stylists and masters. One just tried to tell one's readers in the most dramatic way one could, marshalling the sentences what had happened in the field.

We were treated like an elite—at Madison Square Garden our working press benches bore brass plates with our names upon them; our U.S. Golf Association press badges were of gold; our baseball writers card was a distinction—but it also entailed responsibility to be honest with our readers and ourselves, not to deceive the youth that read us on the score of the heroes they worshipped.

The golden days of the summers of sport passed all too quickly and we were always together: one night with our noses up against the canvas of a ring for a championship fight, the next day looking down from an eyrie-high press box onto a baseball diamond, or collected in the tennis marquee at Forest Hills, or marching some fairway in the wake of Gene Sarazen or Bobby Jones. We met at the Kentucky Derby, the Yale Bowl, Boyle's Thirty Acres, or the Army and Navy game, and there were none of us who did not have writer's nerves as we sat watching for the drama to unfold, knowing that our stories would be the eyes and ears of our readers.

These stories, unforgettable to the narrators as well as to those who read them, knew about or witnessed the events, are in themselves testimony as to why no modern, mechanical, reproducing device will ever replace the dyed-in-the-wool writers of sports tales.

Paul W. Gallico.

CONTENTS

THE
WORKING PRESS

IS IT ONLY A GAME?

by William Saroyan

Written on an assignment for Sports Illustrated *in 1956 by the author-playwright, winner of the 1940 Pulitzer Prize and New York Critics' Circle Award for the* Time of Your Life.

Baseball is caring. Player and fan alike must care, or there is no game. If there's no game, there's no pennant race and no World Series. And for all any of us know there might soon be no nation at all.

The caring is whole and constant, whether warranted or hopeless, tender or angry, ribald or reverent. From the first pitch to the last out the caring continues. With a score of 6–0, two outs, two strikes, nobody on, only an average batter at bat, bottom of the 9th, it is still possible, and sometimes necessary, to believe something can still happen—for the simple reason that it *has* happened before, and very probably will again. And when it does, won't that be the day? Isn't that alone almost enough to live for, assuming there might just be little else? To witness so pure a demonstration of the unaccountable way by which the human spirit achieves stunning, unbelievable grandeur?

If the caring isn't for a team (because a team won't come through, or can't), then it is for the game itself, the annual ritual, moving with time and the world, the carefully planned and slowly accelerated approach to the great reward—the outcome, the answer, the revelation of the best, the winner.

It is good to care—in any dimension. More Americans put their spare (and purest?) caring into baseball than into anything else I can think of—and most of them put at least *a little* of it there. Most of them know the game is going on all the time, like the tides, and suspect there's a reason, or at least wonder about it. What *is* all the fuss about the whole year, and all the excitement every October? *Is* this a nation of kids, or what? Why not existentialism instead of baseball, for instance? Well, for one thing, you've got to be tired to care for old existentialism, and Americans just aren't ready to be that tired yet. For another, baseball can be trusted, as great art can, and bad art can't, especially as it comes from Hollywood, where sharp dealing is an accepted principle of profit-making. And it doesn't matter that baseball is very, very big business—quite the contrary. That only makes its truth all the more touching and magnificent. It doesn't matter, either, that the great players don't think of baseball as I do, for instance. Why should they? It's enough for them to go

11

Take me out to the ball game.

after being great and then to *be* great—and then to be no longer able, as time goes by.

I'm devoted to the game, to all of the teams in both leagues and to the World Series, because I don't know of anything better of its kind to be devoted to—and it's always out there with that anonymous crowd of the hungry and faithful, watching and waiting, in the stadium—their eyes on the geometric design of the fresh diamond, all set for the unfolding of another episode in the great drama, which cannot be put anywhere else—not into movies, not onto the stage, not even onto the television screen (although that's pretty good when you're held captive somewhere 3,000 miles away from the great place and the grand moment), not into books, and not even into statistics, although the game has grown on them.

It's a game—the biggest and best and most decent yet. The idea is to win the most games in the American or the National League, and then to go on and win the World Series: to establish a statistic, and tie it forever to the rag-tag experience of a whole people for a whole year.

I happen to be sorry Cincinnati didn't have the pitching, but they look awfully good for next year. It was great, too, the way Pittsburgh took off early in the season and then came back for a moment near the end and very nearly took the soul out of the Dodgers—but didn't, and that's the important thing as far as the Bums are concerned. I'm sorry, too, that Milwaukee got slugged by St. Louis, but you've got to like the Cardinals, too. You've got to like the game. No team is ever willing to stop caring. The fact is they *can't,* and there is the secret of the game's importance and appeal.

It is a tradition that the President throw out the first ball of the season, but somewhere in the bleachers the poets are around, too.

I don't think you'd get Casey Stengel in any arena of human activity other than baseball, and not getting him would be a national disaster, unbeknownst as it might be. Alston, too—another kind entirely. Bragan. Tebbetts. All of them. Fighting it out with their players and their fans, their friends and enemies, umpires and newspapermen but, most of all, facts and figures—statistics. You don't get Sandy Amoros, either, running in from left field as fast as he can go after an inning in which he dropped one he *had* caught—knowing it might cost the team the pennant. Knowing and waiting, and then hitting and saving the damned pennant, and then fielding and saving it, and then hitting and saving it again—knowing, saying nothing, on the theory (some say) that he doesn't speak much English. That could be it, all right, but there could be another theory, too, and the kids know it, and the old men and the old women know it, and the cab drivers and the cops and people in hospitals and penitentiaries and other lonely places. They don't know Sandy—but what he did, they know *that*. And it's a good thing to know. You wouldn't get Robinson, either—from the beginning. Or Williams, twice back from the wars, or the heroic return of Sal Maglie, and all the others, each made great and more deeply human than ever by the game.

Well, *is* it a game? Is that all it is? So the Dodgers win it again in 1956. So the Yanks win. So what? What good does *that* do the nation? What good does that do the world?

A little good. *Quite* a little.

And there's always next year, too.

LITTLE RED LEGS

by Sir Arthur Conan Doyle—and N.Y. Herald Tribune

The drama of the 1908 Olympic marathon finish by
the creator of the analytical sleuth, Sherlock Holmes.

LONDON, ENGLAND, JULY 25, 1908—Sir Arthur Conan Doyle, in describing the Dorando Scene in the Stadium today said:—

"Thank God he is on his feet again, the little red legs going incoherently, but drumming, hard driven by the supreme will within.

"There is a groan as he falls again, a cheer as he re-staggers to his feet. It is horrible, yet fascinating—this struggle between a set purpose and an utterly exhausted frame. Surely he is done now, he cannot rise again. From under the archway has darted a second runner, Hayes, the stars and stripes on his breast, going gallantly, and well within his strength. There is only 20 yards—if the Italian can do it. He staggers up, no trace of intelligence upon his set face, and again the red legs break into their strange, automatic amble. Will he fall again? No—he sways and balances; then he is through the tape into a score of friendly arms. He has gone to the extreme of human endurance. No Roman of prime ever has borne himself better; the great breed is not yet extinct."

Then, after a tribute to the Americans' splendid performances, and a lament over the Britishers' failure, Sir Arthur Conan Doyle, referring to the Judges' award of the victory to Hayes, says:—"I confess I cannot see how the judges could come to any other decision, and yet the tragedy remains. It was, as matters stood, a fair and square win for the American since, without help, Dorando must have lain senseless on the track."

In his general reference to the American athletes, Sir Arthur says:—"These Americans specialize, and yet they retain the remarkable appearance of all-around excellence. There is no hypertrophy of special muscle; all is symmetry and balance, beauty and grace. The theorist might suppose the evolution of a type meagre in body and powerful in quarters. There is no sign of it."

———

Something struck London today, and the British sportsmen who have active charge of the Olympic Games and the journalists who write predictions for the sporting columns of the London papers will not be able to figure out what it *was* for a week or two. But ten thousand Americans, who formed one-eighth of the record breaking crowd in the Olympic stadium, knew it at once.

It was the fierce victorious scream of the American Eagle, and it smote the ears of the confident prophets of the British successes with more than dismay to think that the Marathon Race, for weeks claimed as Britain's very own, with Canada the only country having a possible look-in, had been won by the "bloody Yankees," and in a style which put their own crack runners in an icebox.

Shades of Boadicea, Alfred, Arthur, George III, to what a pass have the Britons come! All this and more is the feeling of that portion of the British public which has allowed itself to be guided by that sensational portion of Fleet Street which is so pronouncedly anti-American in tone that its main efforts for two weeks have been devoted to stirring up popular feeling against the American athletes.

It was a glorious victory, not only in the Marathon Race, but in the events of the whole day. But this particular race has been the most advertized feature of the whole Games.

The newspapers have been telling all about it, inviting the populace to turn out and see Britain's sons wallop the nether garments off the "blarsted Yanks" and every other nation that had the temerity to enter the lists against them.

People came and saw, but saw the first Britisher to make his appearance in the Stadium in thirteenth place, almost 22 minutes behind John J. Hayes, the American winner, and almost 7 minutes after Towanina, the fourth American to reach home.

Duncan, their vaunted British champion, did not finish at all. Lord, who was also picked for the winner, finished a poor sixteenth and, as for Longboat, the Canadian Indian who was spoken of as a very dark horse, he made his appearance in the Stadium in a wheelbarrow, having given up before the 20th mile.

Perhaps the English critics will blame it on the weather, if they can find no other excuse for the defeat of their men, for it was like a hot July day in the States.

The sun's rays beat down fiercely and there was hardly a breath of air stirring during part of the afternoon. A haze hovered over the Stadium, every nook and cranny of which was filled. The official announcer had donned a long-tailed scarlet coat in honor of the exalted presence of royalty, and the only way the crowd had of keeping cool was to take an occasional look at him every few minutes.

After the start of the Marathon Race from Windsor, he would announce the leaders, and then a man in a white uniform would parade around the arena, bearing a signboard, on which appeared the names of the British runners who were in the van.

At the first mile, two Britons were announced in the lead and the crowd was enthusiastic; at four miles, three Britishers still led; at the ninth, one had been displaced by the South African, Hefferon, and the same men were announced at eighteen miles.

At the nineteenth mile, a feeling of doubt seemed for the first time to strike the spectators when an Italian was announced to be one of the three in the lead. At the twentieth mile, no Englishman was announced. He had given place to number 26, but by the ghost of British fair play this could not be, and they looked at their programmes, rubbed their eyes. "Ah! Hayes, a bloody Yankee."

At three minutes before five o'clock, the course inside the Stadium was cleared. From that time, the vast gathering waited almost breathless. It seemed as if absolute silence had fallen. Then came the announcement that Hefferon of South Africa and Dorando of Italy were leading.

With true British impartiality, the name of Hayes was left out. The crowd at the back of the north end of the stand rose and scanned the road to Windsor. At twenty-four miles, the same announcement was made and bombs were set off.

"What has become of Hayes?" Americans anxiously inquired of each other. To relieve the tension, the Americans in the competitors' stand started to sing. Then, at twenty-three minutes after five o'clock it was announced that Hefferon and Dorando were in sight.

Two minutes later, it was announced that the Italian had entered the grounds and a few minutes later he appeared at the entrance to the Stadium and was greeted by a burst of cheers, but it was immediately perceived that something was wrong. He staggered across the bicycle track, groped blindly forward for a third of the distance to the royal box, and fell. A crowd of officials rushed to him. He was helped up and he started again. In the meantime, twenty yards from the entrance to the grounds, Hayes had overtaken and passed Hefferon. J. M. Andrews, clerk of the course, ran toward the Italian— who had dropped again after another ten yards—and, with a doctor who was accompanying the racer, picked him up.

Dorando reeled across the track like a drunken man, and collapsed again.

Meantime, Hayes had entered the Stadium and was coming on at a fair pace. The officials crowded about Dorando and helped him to his feet and started him again, but a fourth time he staggered and fell. He got upon his feet with difficulty and, with a man on each side of him, was fairly pulled across the line just 21 and 3/5 seconds before Hayes came up.

There never was a pluckier race run, but all in vain. The judges immediately ordered the Italian flag up, and the American was put under it. Meantime, Hefferon had entered the Stadium. He got an ovation, but crossed the line 48 seconds after Hayes, whose official time for the race was 2h. 55m. 18s., an Olympic Marathon record.

Meantime, the American committee had met and lodged a protest on the ground that Dorando had had to be helped to the tape. James E. Sullivan, chairman of the committee, maintained to the officials in charge of the course that they had no right to raise the Italian flag, if they acted consistently with their conduct yesterday when, after Carpenter had won the 400-meters race, he was disqualified and no American flag was raised.

The officials maintained Dorando had not been carried, but the British committee decided to take up the protest at once, and invited the American committee into the conference. The Americans declined on the ground that they had never before been invited to a conference and that it was too late in the day to accept such an invitation.

With a man on each side . . . he was pulled across the line.

"We must leave it," said Mr. Sullivan, "to your sense of justice."

As Hefferon was coming around the track, the crowd had another shock when it discerned that on the breast of the runner who was entering the Stadium was the American shield. This was Forshaw, who crossed the line 1 minute, 4 and 3/5 seconds after Hefferon.

Less than three minutes later, another American shield had burst into sight. It was on little Welton, who came around the track at a great speed, making the finest finish so far.

Then came in succession the three Canadians: Wood, Simpson, and Lawson. Then the Swede, Svanborg and next little Towanina, the American Indian, gamely taking the track on the run, although he looked almost gone.

America had now sent four of her seven entrants across the line among the first ten.

Hatch, of the United States, came in fifteenth, but the other two American entrants, Morrissey and Ryan, dropped out after the twentieth mile.

In all, twenty-seven out of fifty-seven starters finished the race, with Lister of Canada, the last man, reaching the finishing line just about seven o'clock.

Only four of the twelve Englishmen finished as against seven of the dozen Canadian starters.

It was nearly eight o'clock when the British committee made an official announcement that the American protest in regards to the Marathon Race had been upheld, and that the race had been awarded to Hayes. This caused much indignation in the group of judges and unrepresentative British sportsmen who were waiting to hear the results.

I saw little Hayes tonight and, while looking a bit tired, he seemed to be quite happy. "I was behind at the start," he said, "and did not catch the bunch for quite a while. They tell me at the fourteenth mile I was twelfth. I didn't catch Hefferon until three or four miles away when we struck asphalt."

Dorando, who was almost too weak to answer questions when seen tonight, said:—"I felt all right until I entered the Stadium. When I heard the people cheering and knew I had nearly won, a thrill passed through me and I felt my strength going. I fell down, but tried to struggle to the tape, but fell again. I never lost consciousness of what was going on, and if the doctor had not ordered the attendants to pick me up, I believe I could have finished unaided."

Dorando is a confectioner, who resides on the island of Capri. He trained himself for the race without any supervision. He is, however, the Italian long-distance champion, and won the Paris Marathon last year. He hopes to compete again in that race on August 15th.

YEARS LATER

by Ring Lardner

When it came to tongue in cheek, Lardner had no peer. This article on the "Lipton" cup was churned up for those who'd rather weep from laughter.

So FAR AS THE UNDERSIGNED KNOWS, Sir Thomas Lipton is a man of honor whose word is as good as his bond and better than his catboats. Just the same business is business, and it seems to me that before the recent hair-raising yachting contests off Newport are forgotten, it would be a sensible thing to get the old tea-taster to put in writing his verbal promise never to challenge for the Cup again. Otherwise there is a chance that he will send another mash note to the Vanderbilts ten years from now and if they remind him that he had given his word to let us alone, he will say: "Yes, but that was when I was just a kiddie and hadn't learned the facts of life."

Bill Rogers' scheme won't satisfy the old man or me either. Bill suggested that everybody chip in $1.00 apiece and send it to Mayor Walker, whose duty it would be to use the proceeds in the purchase of a consolation cup for Sir Thomas. In the first place, Mr. Lipton lives in a country where you don't have to pour your consolation into a cup even in the main dining room. In the second place, suppose everyone but Bill Rogers did send $1.00 to Mayor Walker; that would only make something like $120,000,000 and the Mayor would face the alternative of being called a cheap skater or paying for the saucer out of his own pocket. In the third place, I understand that Bill is already sorry he conceived the idea; its publication brought him back into the limelight and tore away the blanket of obscurity he has been trying to hide behind for the past fourteen years.

My objections to the Lipton Cup races are several. Chief among them is that they invariably cast a pall of gloom over the American people, gloom so contagious that even I, ordinarily equipped with an irresistible smile of good-fellowship for everybody, feel like hell from the moment a new Shamrock's barnacle is sighted off Muscle Shoals until at least a month after someone has called up the garage and had it towed back to Edinburgh. This depression of soul is generally attributed to our spirit of sportsmanship; we hate to see such a good fellow lose when he is so anxious to triumph, and so game. (His sorrowful words brokenly uttered during the last day at Newport—"I cannot win! I cannot win!"—left hardly a dry eye in any American speakeasy and will go down in history along with

such famous slogans as Gridley's "Don't fire till you are damn good and ready!" and Admiral Schley's "I can't get them to go home!") The facts are, I think, that about ten Americans are acquainted with Sir Thomas and only six or seven are well enough acquainted with him to know whether he is a good fellow. As for his anxiety to triumph, I believe if that were on the level he would either have Gar Wood build him a boat or challenge the Philadelphia National League baseball team.

It seems to me the actual cause of gloom is that the defense of the Cup is in the hands of an exclusive yacht club and everybody hates an exclusive yacht club. What makes it exclusive is that you have to have a yacht to belong to it. Around New York and other cities, even cities where there is no water except the lavatory, you can find plenty of yacht clubs with members who would rather jump out of a twelfth-story window than look at a picture of the Europa. But a yacht club that bars you unless you own at least a canoe is a snooty organization which a large majority of us would love to see humiliated even by a Greek.

And then I object to the way our newspapers treat these feverish events. They spread them all over the front page and crowd out things you want to read, that are really news, such as the natural death of somebody in New Jersey. The lead stories are written by experts who carry along a pocket dictionary to refer to in case they forget the difference between a yawl and a squall. From the front page, the stories are jumped, for some whimsical reason, to the sporting section, where they are illustrated by photographs of the challenger and the defender (you can instantly tell which is which by reading the captions), and accompanied by several columns of sidelights under the signatures of special writers who wish, before the first limb of the course is covered, that they had been sent to the morgue, and will soon get their wish. The experts, or their managing editors, receive poison-pen letters from members of the yacht club because they made some technical error, like saying the winning boat lost, and the special writers are never again worth a damn and spend the balance of their lives meeting doctors.

I do not claim (except when I am all by myself in a room) that I was worth a damn to begin with, but I do know that the Lipton Cup "race" of 1920 is what is the matter with my stomach today. I was assigned to sidelights and accepted the assignment with pleasure, as I really love dat ole davil sea and thought the job would cure me of the effects of the Democratic Convention in San Francisco, which was something of a strain on the abdomen.

Well, the newspaper boys were conveyed to and from the scene each day on U.S. destroyers, and the schedule was like this: You showed up at a certain pier in North River at five in the a.m. and got on a tug. The tug took you out to within eight feet of the destroyer (ours was the Semmes) and you covered the eight feet from the tug to the destroyer by walking a tight rope. When I am in the best of health and have had a good night's sleep, it is all I can do to keep from

. . . the old tea-taster's catboat, off Newport.

falling off the Boardwalk at Atlantic City. So when it was necessary to stay up till five o'clock so I would be up at five o'clock and then start the day with an eight-foot stroll on a piece of wire, I was all primed to turn out a column of sidelights that would keep readers in gales of silence.

As you will recall, the event was held off Sandy Hook that year. It started in August in a .02-mile wind and ended in February with the Shamrock defeated but still ahead. The Semmes had to stay in reverse to keep up with the flying contestants. I watched the entire orgy from a sleeping position in the lieutenant's bunk after leaving a call for 4:30 p.m. which was the usual time that the official statement, "No race," was given out.

When it became necessary for Sir Thomas to start back home and participate in the St. Patrick's Day pep meetings, we special writers gradually resumed contact with the world and discovered that many changes had taken place. Harding had been elected president, the European war was over, Herman Rosenthal had eaten some bad oysters, and my family had moved from Garden City to Great Neck.

Proponents of international cup racing point out that that race, held a decade ago, accomplished some good in a scientific way. They claim that the photographs taken of the two yachts in action were the origin of slow-motion pictures. But I would gladly trade that discovery for my good old digestive apparatus. And I say again that Sir Thomas should be made to put his promise in writing. Or else that the 1940 race be started in the Niagara River, just above those old Falls.

THE HAVANA AFFAIR

by Damon Runyon

*"Always a sucker for a heavyweight fighter," Runyon, in addition
to inventing a new language, covered every championship held
during his lifetime, starting with this one in 1915.*

HAVANA, APRIL 5—Tonight, Jess Willard, a gawky, green-looking Kansas
farmer cowpuncher, is champion heavyweight of the world, with all the world
before him, while Jack Johnson, late lord of the pugilistic realm, is just a
portly middle-aged colored man, browsing on the memory of one of the greatest
battles ever made by a fighter of his years.

One ferocious right-hand smash to the pit of Johnson's fat stomach, that
crumpled the body of the Negro in grinding pain at the opening of the twenty-
sixth round, followed less than a minute and a half later by a terrific right-hand
clip to the jaw, are blows that made new history for American sport on alien
soil this afternoon.

With alien tongues drowning the sound of American voices in the weird
demonstration that followed, Johnson fell and was counted out by referee
Jack Welch in Willard's corner.

For twenty-five rounds, the Negro had battled bitterly and bravely against
this gigantic young white opponent, waging a warfare of such gameness and
craft as to finally arouse the admiration of even the sporting men at the ringside who have been waiting since 1910 for this day.

And, while the finish was obvious, no one looked for it so soon. Only
the round before, some one in the crowd remarked that Johnson had quit
laughing. Johnson turned, winked his eye and lifted his bruised and bloody
lips in the ghost of his famous old "golden smile," then stumbled out of his
corner for the twenty-sixth round.

Willard met him with that lifting smash in a neutral corner, the blow
driving through the Negro's guard. Johnson was badly hurt and dropped both
hands completely, but quickly pushed them up again before him. The memory
of that murderous smash was ever uppermost in his mind during the next
eighty seconds as he shuffled wearily around the ring, and it was probably a
repetition of that wallop that he was trying to avoid when he was knocked out.

He backed over into Willard's corner, where Willard feinted as if to
again whip his right into the paunchy cushion across the black man's middle.

25

Johnson once more lowered his guard, trying to get away, and the next instant the massive gloved right fist of the Kansan crashed into the black jaw.

Johnson dropped flat on his back, without scarcely staggering. Even referee Jack Welch seemed stunned with surprise when the big black toppled over, but he quickly began counting over the dark form that lay with face upturned to the sun of a dying afternoon; and just as the withered hand of the old referee toiled on the finish of a champion, the crowd made a wild rush for the ring, with the Americans in the van.

Johnson did not seem to be totally unconscious, recovering soon after his seconds had gathered him up. He stood a minute in the centre of the ring with a white towel wrapped around his black face, blinking his eyes at the sun and listening to the roar about him; then he went to his corner.

Meantime, Willard would have been lost in the great swarm in his corner but for his great height. The big farmer grinned amiably while frenzied men reached for his hand. The Cuban soldiers had to pile into the ring with drawn sabres to rescue both fighters from the crush.

When Jack Curley went over to Johnson's corner to cut the gloves off his hands, the Negro looked up, smiled feebly, and said, "Let me keep these."

"How do you feel?" asked Curley.

"All right," said Johnson. "Everything is all right; the best man won."

Later, Johnson told Tom Flanagan he was glad he lost. He said:

"Now all my troubles will be over. They will let me alone."

Johnson knew he was gone sooner than anybody else. In the rest between the twenty-first and twenty-second rounds he sent for H. H. Frazee and asked him to find Curley. Soon afterwards, he told Flanagan he was getting weak and could not last much longer.

"I want you to get my wife out of here," he said.

Flanagan told him to go on a few rounds and see how he felt. Between the twenty-fifth and twenty-sixth, Curley was found.

Johnson repeated his request to him. Curley went to the box occupied by Mrs. Johnson, back of Willard's corner, and told her what Jack said. He offered to take her out. Mrs. Johnson agreed to go.

The twenty-sixth round had started when she arose. As she moved past Willard's corner the knockout came. Her husband dropped before her eyes.

She exclaimed, "Oh, my God," then disappeared in the mad crush of 18,000 people suddenly gone mad.

Something approaching a race riot followed. Thousands of people began parading the race track, yelling "Viva la Blanca," while the blacks drew off in little groups. The Cuban cavalry, which had finished fighting their way to Willard, drew up in close formation to quell any real trouble, but the people finally dispersed.

When autos were coming in from the track with first news, thousands of men and women, and even children, lined the streets roaring approval. The chauffeur who drove the first car to leave the track flew along, handling the car with one hand and the other holding up a picture of Willard, while even the traffic policemen gave him a cheer.

Tonight the town buzzes with elation over the victory. While Americans join with the Cubans in rejoicing, they do not hesitate to give Johnson full praise for his fight.

Prominent ring followers were not ashamed to be seen shaking the hand of the old black, during the jam about his corner at the finish. He fought a masterly battle and wonder is he was able to last as long as he did, for the result has been regarded here as an almost foregone conclusion for days.

Without taking anything from Willard's victory, few believe he would have had the slightest chance with Johnson a few years back.

It was a battle of one lone black man against the whole world, so to speak. Fat, ill-conditioned, harassed by anathemas from people in the crowd, with age obviously tugging throughout, Johnson nevertheless fought along with marvelous craft against this crude but amazingly powerful young opponent.

Willard was a big surprise. It is true, Johnson has gone far back, but Willard outboxed him and outroughed him all the way. His abnormal height gave him some advantage over Johnson, but his strength was his main asset. He fought carefully, as he said he would, with Tom Jones whispering instructions in his ear between rounds.

While still far from being a finished fighter perhaps, he was anything but as awkward as some expected to see him.

Johnson did not talk as much to Willard as used to be his custom with other opponents. He had little to say to the crowd. Whenever he spoke to Jess it was good-naturedly. Jess answered in monosyllables. Only once did Jack answer a remark from the crowd with any heat; but the old "golden smile" rarely broke across his countenance. He frequently nodded to acquaintances in the crowd between rounds, but his whole attitude indicated depression.

Johnson said tonight he is going back to Paris. He expects his interests in the pictures will bring him an income.

The gate receipts today approximated $160,000.

While the twentieth round was being fought, Jack Curley took compassion on the frenzied throngs at the gates and admitted them at a dollar per head, but the dollar went to "Curley" Brown as admission to the races which followed the fight.

Each left the track at once and returned to town. Willard was only slightly marked, while Johnson showed no bruises of the battle.

Probably never before has there been a heavyweight championship battle where advance opinion was so general as on the result of this one. That stout stomach of Johnson's was largely responsible, but even before, it was apparent the Negro could not get into condition.

The members of the syndicate which controls Willard had been sending telegrams to friends in the States urging them to bet on the white man. Despite this feeling there was not much betting. Even today, most of the wagers were small. Pari-mutuel machines at the track paid 5 to 6 on Willard. After the tenth round, Willard was a strong favorite. One man bet 8 to 1 Willard would win inside of twenty-five rounds.

Willard's own description of the finish is about as has been recorded. He says Johnson seemed to be in deadly fear of another stomach punch from the time he got a blow at the opening of the last relief, and that he intended to keep pounding away at that point until he saw the opening for the jaw.

The fight promoters are talking of a special train to take Willard back to New York, but Jess is still most happy in the company of two friends from Kansas.

Jess suffered his greatest surprise today immediately after the fight, when two Cubans rushed up and kissed him with resounding smacks on the cheeks.

The ring was erected right under the finish wire in the home stretch of Curley Brown's race track, which is located in a pleasant valley surrounded by gently rising little hills and topped by waving palms.

Some of the cheaper seats were as far away from the ring as the quarter pole. The higher priced chairs were set on the ground right up against the platform on which the ring was pitched.

Beginning as early as 11 o'clock, the roads leading to the track were filled with racing motors that left only white streaks of dust behind. There are no specified motor laws in Cuba, so the drivers made it a grand race. Despite the frequent patrols of mounted police, there were numerous accidents.

It was partially cloudy all morning, with a hint of rain, but toward noon the skies began clearing and the sun broke forth in the boxes close to the ring, where there were numerous handsomely gowned women, both Americans and Cubans, with Cubans predominating.

The crowd was rather silent, compared to what an American crowd would have been under the same circumstances. Joking, characteristic of Americans, was wholly lacking.

At 1:15, there was a great stir throughout the field and a wild babble of voices as Johnson came tramping down the aisle, looking like an old Moor, in a black and white striped robe which just showed his grinning face and egg-shaped, closely shaven head.

The champion climbed into the ring and gazed out over the throng, talking to Tom Flanagan, while Jack Curley came in and piled a set of new chocolate-colored gloves in the centre of the ring. A pair of scales had been carried into the ring, and Curley Brown leaped upon the platform under the pretense of being wanted to examine the scales, and was introduced by Mace, who had regained the megaphone of authority from Rosenthal.

Black Bob Armstrong and blacker Sam McVey followed Johnson, carrying pails and sponges. Australian Colin Beli and Dave Mills were Johnson's other handlers. When Johnson tried to sit in an ordinary kitchen chair in the corner, he found it too small, and Armstrong knocked off the back. Oldtimers remembered the same thing had to be done with Sullivan at New Orleans.

Willard entered while the dismembering of the chair was going on, and received a great greeting. The long Kansan was attired in a maroon sweater and a pair of blue street pants, which he stripped off immediately. Johnson stepped on the scales first, throwing off his robe and showing a pair of light blue trunks, while Willard wore tights of a darker blue hue and an American flag around his waist.

Miss Cecilia Wright, an English singer who has appeared in New York theatres, was sitting at the press bench to write a story for several local American papers. Johnson took exception to her presence, and said he would not fight until she was excluded from the box. Johnson's reason was that he did not want women to hear what he might have to say. Miss Wright took a seat farther back without protest.

Willard's weight was announced at 238 pounds, Johnson's 225. During the introduction of Tom Jones, Willard lolled back in his chair, his great limbs stretched out before him, and kept licking his lips.

"Now all my troubles will be over. They will let me alone."

Johnson's expression never changed one iota during these preliminaries. His sleepy eyes were narrowed to slits as he let his gaze stray over the crowd. He gave his wife a brief nod of recognition.

When Willard was introduced, he received a tremendous demonstration from the crowd, which now stretched all over the inclosure. Willard's seconds were Tom Jones, Jim Savage, "Tex" O'Rourke and Walter Monahan. At 1:27 Curley yelled, "Clear the ring!" and everybody piled out. Referee Welch nodded to Bob Vernon, who whacked the big gong with a hammer, and the fight was on.

Both men walked out of their corners slowly, Johnson being especially deliberate. After a brief bit of sparring that had no result one way or the other, they went into a clinch. For the first time, Johnson's celebrated "golden smile" beamed across his face. But the once bright teeth were now dimmed and broken where the gold has disappeared.

Willard pumped three stout blows to Johnson's paunch without much effect. Johnson nodded sleepily when Welch called the men to break. Perspiration broke out on the shiny head of the Negro almost immediately. His body was soon as wet and slippery as a seal's but, oddly enough, as the fight went along, the sweat gradually disappeared and, at the finish, the Negro's body was perfectly dry. This was probably due to the way Jack rested through the closing rounds.

When the first round, which was fairly even, ended, there came the first uproar, the Cubans being especially demonstrative and filling the air with screams of "Viva!" for one man or the other. From Americans came yells of encouragement for Willard. Hardly one English voice was heard in Johnson's behalf, although some of the Cubans cried his name. Never for a moment did Willard seem afraid of his dusky opponent.

In the second round, the long Kansan led briskly for the stomach, and throughout the fight kept striding in without fear. It was in the second round that Johnson began a series of statuesque poses that he kept up to the end.

He would stand perfectly still with gloves poised high in the air and eyes glued to Willard for several seconds at a stretch. It was probably his way of resting. Willard staggered him slightly in this round with a body rip, and it became apparent to all that the Negro had lost his speed. He shuffled about the ring.

Johnson got in a smash to Willard's stomach that caused Jess's mouth to pop open, but when the second round came to a close, Jess was still marching in unafraid.

Up to this time, Johnson had not said a word. He rarely smiled. Verbal abuse fell on him from all sides of the ring, but he gave no sign that he heard them until the third round, when he made some remark to Willard when he sat down in his chair between rounds.

It was noticed Johnson breathed heavily, but in the fourth he deliberately thrust his stomach forward inviting a blow from Jess. Willard's blocking was excellent, and he always seemed to have perfect command of himself at all times, standing on tip-toe to make Johnson hit high.

Willard's lips began bleeding in the fourth. Later on, blood smears showed on his right ear, while Johnson spat blood between the rounds.

In the sixth, Johnson began making a desperate effort to put some drive behind his punches; but when that round closed, the waist band of his trunks was imbedded in a thick roll of fat when he breathed.

Old Jack was showing the effect of the grind, but in the next round he made a desperate charge that brought Jess's tongue between his teeth. Johnson missed one swing that almost overbalanced him.

Johnson started rushing the big Kansan in the seventh, and finally worked him against the ropes. Willard finally got his long left jab working to perfection and temporarily blinded the Negro's left eye. Johnson then came back with a series of swings to Willard's body.

Willard seemed to be gaining more and more confidence and in the eighth started off by forcing the pace. A wild exchange started in the middle of this round and the Negro usually beat the white man to the punch. Johnson finally got to close quarters and brought up a hard right uppercut to the jaw.

This punch sent Willard spinning against the ropes and as he bounded back he ran into a left to the jaw. Then he gave Johnson in return a hard straight left to the face. As the bell rang, Johnson was pumping both hands to the head.

Johnson wore a worried look as the ninth passed and the tenth came, and which was about the time the fight commenced to slow up. He shambled out of his corner wiping the sweat from his eyes and casting a queer, dumb look upward to the sun and outward over the crowd.

High overhead swung a number of Cuban buzzards with wings flattened against the sky and beaks drooped. The crowd had grown quiet for a moment, and only the voice of a Cuban was heard passing through the boxes, offering to bet on Johnson, when suddenly an American well back from the ring rose and thundered an offer of $500 to $400 on the Kansan.

"This is the round," said Jack, as he walked back after the tenth, but the meaning of his comment was not apparent during the eleventh. He was constantly talking and answering remarks hurled at him from the crowd. Once he said something to Willard that made Jess grin at the finish of the round. He playfully slapped Jess on his back and the great, hairy body of the white man was red from punches. His leg muscles were shaking like masses of jelly, but Jess did not seem in the least fatigued. His eyes were bright and wide open.

The eyes of the Negro were heavy with great weariness. Lying back in his chair, his stomach was as flabby as a mass of black dough and it was an effort for his seconds to push their hands between the waistband and his body to aid his breathing.

The faces of the old followers of the game grouped around the ring were

YANKEES TOSS GAME AWAY IN THIRTEENTH

The New York Times

From The New York Times *of 1912. Written by a non-byline writer who should have had one.*

Here's one that will bring the weeps.

The Yankees and the Athletics were tied in the thirteenth inning at 4 to 4. Rube Oldring jarred Ford's damp hurl to the center lawn for a single. Ford's next moist fling slipped and went wild, Oldring racing to second, and then to third. Gabby Street recovered the unruly ball, made a desperate heave to Coleman at third base, and the ball traveled on to left field, Oldring coming home with the run which won the game. Score, 5 to 4.

Play on, professor—a little more of that funeral march.

Some 3500 persons, mostly men, sat through to the bitter end, and everyone got cold smoked beef when he walked into the Missus for dinner at 7:30 last evening. That wasn't all they got.

This is the conversation, husband speaking: "Say, Mrs. Wife, you ought to have seen that pitching duel between Bender and Ford. The Yanks tied it up in the sixth, and after that both flingers were airtight."

Mrs. Wife now talking: "Say, you, what do you think this is—an all-night lunch? Why don't you board up at the ball park? You'll find something to eat at the 'Ham-And' place around the corner."

It was a ball game worth missing your dinner for. The Yankees showed more fight and vim than in any game this season. For a long time they refused to be whipped, and their chances were just as good as the world's champions until they cracked in the thirteenth inning and began to toss the ball all over the lot. Wolverton's men had several excellent chances to win the game, but they lacked the final punch.

The Yankees are in pretty bad shape, and had to rely on green recruits to fill the gaps made by the hospital patients. The whole outfield is now disabled, Hartzell being yesterday's victim, while Cree and Walter are still recuperating.

In the second inning, Daniels in center and Hartzell in right both chased after Bender's high fly. The players came together with an awful bump, and Hartzell stretched out on the grass, unconscious. A gash was cut in his chin, and he was carried to the clubhouse. Benny Kauff took his place, and was all hot sand and ginger in the game. Kauff made two fine hits and ran the bases fast, scoring two of the Yankee runs.

It was a toss-up between Bender and Ford. Both pitched great after the sixth inning, getting stronger as they went along. It was the first big game the big Chippewa Indian has pitched since the World Series last fall, and he looks as if he were good for a couple more World Series. Ford was back to his best form and, with men on the bases, was very effective. Ragged support behind him aided the Athletics in their run harvest.

Philadelphia activity started in the second. Murphy was safe when Martin threw wild to Chase at first. McInnis beat out a bunt to Ford, and Barry sacrificed

And everyone got cold smoked beef for dinner.

the pair up a notch. Then, who comes along but Ira Thomas, who wallops a "pippin" to deep center for a zwei hassocks, scoring Murphy and McInnis. The Yanks got one in that stanza, when Kauff ripped a single to center, went down to second on Zinn's out, and scored on Gardner's hit to the middle patch.

In the fourth, Barry did a brazen piece of business. Murphy singled, went to second on McInnis's out and to third on a passed ball. Barry's roller went to Coleman, and Murphy was nailed while skipping up and down the third base line, Barry racing around to third, while half a dozen Yankees riveted their attention on Murphy. As Ford was pitching to Thomas, Barry started down the third base line like a runaway colt.

The mammoth nerve of him! The grand larceny was committed with all the Yankees looking on with their baby-blue eyes wide open. Barry slid in safe, while the Yankees continued the nap. Get out the alarm clock.

In the fifth, Oldring was safe on a rap which skinned Gardner's shins, and he scored on Collins's double to right. In the same inning, the Yankees began to rush up from behind. Gardner singled and Street strolled. Ford sacrificed them along a base, and they both tore home on Daniels' safe smash to center.

Sixth inning—Yanks at bat, two out. Benny Kauff banged out a safety to right and went to second when Murphy juggled the ball. Kauff scored on Zinn's single to center. The score is tied. Nifty, what?

Ford and Bender both closed up like morning glories in the sun. At nine innings, not a run in sight. Tenth inning, the same thing. In the eleventh inning, Collins walked on Ford's only pass of the day, and got to third on two outs. He stuck there as if planted in glue.

The Yankees should have won in the twelfth inning. Young Martin, the new shortstopper whom Wolverton has just recalled from Rochester, poled a high-powered three-bagger to the darkest corner of right field. He had plenty of time to make the circuit, but was held at third base because of poor coaching. It was a burning shame that such a healthy smash could go to seed, but Martin was tagged coming in on Zinn's grounder.

Then followed the fitful thirteenth, when the strong-armed pegs of Ford and Street permitted Oldring to breeze home with the hurrah tally.

SPORT FOR ART'S SAKE

by Heywood Broun

A prodigious writer, an unsuccessful candidate for Congress, "a mountain of a man, physically and intellectually." He died in 1939. This was written in 1921.

FOR YEARS WE HAD BEEN HEARING about moral victories and at last we saw one. This is not intended as an excuse for the fact that we said before the fight that Carpentier would beat Dempsey. We erred with Bernard Shaw. The surprising revelation which came to us on this July afternoon was that a thing may be done well enough to make victory entirely secondary. We have all heard, of course, of sport for sport's sake but Georges Carpentier established a still more glamorous ideal. Sport for art's sake was what he showed us in the big wooden saucer over on Boyle's dirty acres.

It was the finest tragic performance in the lives of ninety thousand persons. We hope that Professor George Pierce Baker sent his class in dramatic composition. We will be disappointed if Eugene O'Neill, the white hope of the American drama, was not there. Here for once was a laboratory demonstration of life. None of the crowds in Greece who went to somewhat more beautiful stadia in search of Euripides ever saw the spirit of tragedy more truly presented. And we will wager that Euripides was not able to lift his crowd up upon its hind legs into a concerted shout of "Medea! Medea! Medea!" as Carpentier moved the fight fans over in Jersey City in the second round. In fact it is our contention that the fight between Dempsey and Carpentier was the most inspiring spectacle which America has seen in a generation.

Personally we would go further back than that. We would not accept a ticket for David and Goliath as a substitute. We remember that in that instance the little man won, but it was a spectacle less fine in artistry from the fact that it was less true to life. The tradition that Jack goes up the beanstalk and kills his giant, and that Little Red Ridinghood has the better of the wolf, and many other stories are limited in their inspirational quality by the fact that they are not true. They are stories that man has invented to console himself on winter's evenings for the fact that he is small and the universe is large. Carpentier showed us something far more thrilling. All of us who watched him know now that man cannot beat down Fate, no matter how much his will may flame, but he can rock it back upon its heels when he puts all his heart and his shoulders into a blow.

That is what happened in the second round. Carpentier landed his straight right upon Dempsey's jaw and the champion, who was edging in toward him, shot back and then swayed forward. Dempsey's hands dropped to his side. He was an open target. Carpentier swung a terrific right-hand uppercut and missed. Dempsey fell into a clinch and held on until his head cleared. He kept close to Carpentier during the rest of the fight and wore him down with body blows during the infighting. We know of course that when the first prehistoric creature

. . . at last, a moral victory . . . a laboratory demonstration of life.

crawled out of the ooze up to the beaches (see *The Outline of History* by H. G. Wells, some place in the first volume, just a couple of pages after that picture of the big lizard) it was already settled that Carpentier was going to miss that uppercut. And naturally it was inevitable that he should have the worst of it at infighting. Fate gets us all in the clinches, but Eugene O'Neill and all our young writers of tragedy make a great mistake if they think that the poignancy of the fate of man lies in the fact that he is weak, pitiful and helpless. The tragedy of life is not that man loses but that he almost wins. Or, if you are intent on pointing out that his downfall is inevitable, that at least he completes the gesture of being on the eve of victory.

For just eleven seconds on the afternoon of July 2 we felt that we were at the threshold of a miracle. There was such flash and power in that right-hand thrust of Carpentier's that we believed Dempsey would go down, and that fate would go with him and all the plans laid out in the days of the oozy friends of Mr. Wells. No sooner were the men in the ring together than it seemed just as certain that Dempsey would win as that the sun would come up on the morning of July 3. By and by we were not so sure about the sun. It might be down, we thought, and also out. It was included in the scope of Carpentier's punch, we feared. No, we did not exactly fear it. We respect the regularity of the universe by which we live, but we do not love it. If the blow had been as devastating as we first believed, we should have counted the world well lost.

Great circumstances produce great actors. History is largely concerned with arranging good entrances for people; and later exits not always quite as good. Carpentier played his part perfectly down to the last side. People who saw him just as he came before the crowd reported that he was pitifully nervous, drawn, haggard. It was the traditional and becoming nervousness of the actor just before a great performance. It was gone the instant Carpentier came in sight of his ninety thousand. His head was back and his eyes and his smile flamed as he crawled through the ropes. And he gave some curious flick to his bathrobe as he turned to meet the applause. Until that very moment we had been for Dempsey, but suddenly we found ourself up on our feet making silly noises. We shouted, "Carpentier! Carpentier! Carpentier!" and forgot even to be ashamed of our pronunciation. He held his hands up over his head and turned until the whole arena, including the five-dollar seats, had come within the scope of his smile.

Dempsey came in a minute later and we could not cheer, although we liked him. It would have been like cheering for Niagara Falls at the moment somebody was about to go over in a barrel. Actually there is a difference of sixteen pounds between the two men, which is large enough, but it seemed that afternoon as if it might have been a hundred. And we knew for the first time that a man may smile and smile and be an underdog.

We resented at once the law of gravity, the Malthusian theory and the fact that a straight line is the shortest distance between two points. Everything scientific, exact, and inevitable was distasteful. We wanted the man with the curves to win.

It seemed impossible throughout the first round. Carpentier was first out of his corner and landed the first blow, a light but stinging left to the face. Then Dempsey closed in and even the people who paid only thirty dollars for their seats could hear the thump, thump of his short hooks as they beat upon the narrow stomach of Carpentier. The challenger was only too evidently tired when the round ended.

Then came the second and, after a moment of fiddling about, he shot his right hand to the jaw. Carpentier did it again, a second time, and this was the blow perfected by a lifetime of training. The time was perfect, the aim was perfect, every ounce of strength was in it. It was the blow which had downed Bombardier Wells, and Joe Beckett. It rocked Dempsey to his heels, but it broke Carpentier's hand. His best was not enough. There was an earthquake in Philistia but then out came the signs "Business as usual!" and Dempsey began to pound Carpentier in the stomach.

The challenger faded quickly in the third round, and in the fourth the end came. We all suffered when he went down the first time, but he was up again, and the second time was much worse. It was in this knockdown that his head sagged suddenly, after he struck the floor, and fell back upon the canvas. He was conscious and his legs moved a little, but they would not obey him. A gorgeous human will had been beaten down to a point where it would no longer function.

If you choose, that can stand as the last moment in a completed piece of art. We are sentimental enough to wish to add the tag that after a few minutes Carpentier came out to the center of the ring and shook hands with Dempsey and at that moment he smiled again the same smile which we had seen at the beginning of the fight when he stood with his hands above his head. Nor is it altogether sentimental. We feel that one of the elements of tragedy lies in the fact that Fate gets nothing but the victories and the championships. Gesture and glamor remain with Man. No infighting can take that away from him.

Jack Dempsey won fairly and squarely. He is a great fighter, perhaps the most efficient the world has ever known, but everybody came away from the arena talking about Carpentier. He wasn't very efficient. The experts say he fought an ill-considered fight and should not have forced it. In using such a plan, they say, he might have lasted the whole twelve rounds. That was not the idea. As somebody has said, "Better four rounds of—" but we can't remember the rest of the quotation.

Dempsey won and Carpentier got all the glory. Perhaps we will have to enlarge our conception of tragedy, for that too is tragic.

THAT
WAS THE DAY

UNDER FOUR MINUTES

by Arthur Daley

The breaking of trackdom's magic barrier as reported by The New York Times'
long standing favorite and Pulitzer Prize winner of 1956.

IT FINALLY HAPPENED. The 4-minute mile no longer is an impenetrable barrier. Roger Bannister of England burst through it and beyond with his electri-
fying 3:59.4 yesterday under conditions that would seem to make its acceptance
as a world record a formality. From an athletic standpoint this is as historic as
the breaking of the sound barrier.

In the enthusiasm of the moment, there is a tendency to rank Bannister's
exploit as the most important sports achievement of this century. Yet it may
still hold that stature even after sober and profound reflection. Casey Stengel's
pet adjective fits it perfectly. It is truly "tree-mendous."

Trackdom's Holy Grail was within his reach . . .

To foot racers, the 4-minute mile was what Mount Everest was to mountain climbers, a defiant peak that could not be successfully assailed. But someone finally reached the top of Everest and someone also has scaled the peak of the 4-minute mile.

The surprising aspects of this feat are two in number. In most ratings of the world's best milers, Bannister was third on the totem pole behind John Landy of Australia and Wes Santee of the United States. The Aussie had done 4:02 and had five other performances under 4:03. The Kansan had done 4:02.4 while Bannister's best official mark was 4:02.6, since his paced mile of 4:02 had been disallowed. Yet the paced effort demonstrated that the ability was there and that trackdom's Holy Grail was within his reach.

The second surprise developed in the circumstances of the race. The experts had insisted all along that the 4-minute mile could be surpassed only under perfect conditions. The track itself would have to be perfect. So would the weather and so would the running of the race itself. But reports from Britain reveal that a strong cross wind blew across the track and that sullen clouds hung overhead. "Conditions are stupid," remarked Bannister beforehand. Yet they didn't seem to trouble him.

About the "cross wind" item . . . when a race is run around an oval track, it has no effect on the acceptability of a record. It blows against a runner just as much as it blows behind him. Technically speaking, the buffeting he gets from a wind takes so much out of him that the helping tailwind cannot compensate.

However, the competition was ideal. Chris Brasher set a blistering first half and then faded while Chris Chataway, the top-flight British Olympian, challenged the rangy medical student enough to force him all out on the final lap. No time was wasted in jockeying or maneuvering for position, a significant consideration. Thus was Gunder (the Wonder) Haegg's mile record of 4:01.4 sunk without a trace.

Almost two months ago, a feature story from Stockholm appeared in this newspaper. In it Gunder the Wonder was quoted as predicting that Bannister was his choice to be the first to crack the 4-minute mile. Some of his quotes are worth repeating:

"Bannister has brains. That's something you can't say about all runners. He doesn't over-train the way most runners do. You don't see Bannister burning himself out, running twenty and thirty miles a day. He's a miler, a middle-distance man. That's the way he trains. He makes his daily session as much like a mile race or a series of middle-distance races as he can."

However, Haegg erred slightly in saying that the Briton would need stadium walls to block off any wind. But he was correct in declaring that the runner must not be "psychologically tied down—afraid of the mighty 4-minute mile."

That's why it was a trifle disconcerting to have Landy, the Australian, express those fears when he arrived in Stockholm the other day for a competitive tour.

"It will be very hard to run a mile in 4 minutes or less," he said. "It's just that last little bit that matters."

and he reached it.

Landy obviously was wearing those psychological fears Haegg mentioned. Bannister was not. So he broke the record.

Somehow or other a feeling of smug satisfaction follows the news that mile supremacy has returned to Britain, where it originated. They don't have the coaches over there that we have here, and the sports attitude in general has been "jolly well done, old chap." English casualness is almost alarming to intense Americans.

That makes the Bannister achievement a monumental personal accomplishment. It was his first race of the year and he did it all himself with typical British doggedness. Being a medical student, he had to steal his training hours where he could find them.

There will be many miles henceforth under 4 minutes. The impossible no longer is out of reach. Even Bannister's record will be broken some day. But never will it be forgotten that he was the first to reach into the realm of fantasy and surpass the 4-minute mile.

FIRST WORLD SERIES

by John R. Tunis

*Famous for his coverage of tennis immortals, the
author wrote this classic short-short in 1958.*

"The Ohio Farmer," as the sports writers liked to call him because he came from a small farm in Ohio, was then thirty-six, with the large heart of a champion. The night before the opener, when the Boston fans assailed the Pirate players in the lobby of the Hotel Vendome where the visitors were staying, shouting that the Pilgrims would clean them up, Honus Wagner, the great Pittsburgh shortstop, retorted:

"Who with? That old man?"

Yet that "old" man was a toughie. Cy Young pitched the first perfect game in the majors: no hits, no runs, nobody to reach first. There have only been three others since his day. In twenty-two years he won 511 games, more than any other pitcher in baseball ever has won, or ever will. When he finally quit the game in 1911, at the age of forty-four, it was because a young rookie beat him by a score of 1 to 0.

"Time to stop," he said, after this game. The rookie was an unknown youngster named Grover Cleveland Alexander.

In that first Series Young lost the opener to the great Deacon Phillippi of the Pirates, 7 to 3, pitched six innings of the third game, won the fifth, 11 to 2, and three days later the seventh, 7 to 3. Besides being a superb pitcher, he batted .341 in forty-one games that season.

Cy was one of our heroes, and we were as amazed as the other fans to see him calmly sitting behind the window selling tickets. The crowd had come so fast and was so large that extra ticket booths had been hastily erected, and as no other help was at hand, the Boston management sent out the early arrivals among the players to sell seats. Drawing near, we observed the careless manner in which Cy scooped bills from the counter and shoved them onto the floor.

Reaching the window at last, we discovered all standing room gone. Only a few fifty-cent seats remained, and we had no extra money save our trolley fare home. Should we pool resources and one of us go in? While we stood, unhappy, debating, and the fans behind us grew restless, the kind man who had rescued my young brother leaned over and slapped down a bill.

"Give them both seats, Cy," he said. A miracle had happened, so, clutching our tickets with joy, we went eagerly through the gate in delight with our benefactor, and discovered the seats were directly back of first base. It would be impossible, of course, to get seats like this on the morning of a Series game today.

What difference would you, as a modern fan, have observed in that game fifty years and more ago? For one thing, you would immediately have noticed a difference in the crowd. First, there were no women present. Then, every man was in his Sunday best, in black suits and black derbies, with no white shirts visible. Next, you would realize at once that these people were fans, the forgotten men in modern baseball. They had followed the team all summer, knew every player, recognized them, and called down to them by name.

One of the more regrettable features of the present income-tax law is the clause allowing deductions for corporate entertainment. As a result, the World Series has become, in the words of Morris Ernst, New York tax lawyer, "Probably the greatest single tax-deductible item ever practiced in the history of man. Corporations invite guests, supply tickets, transportation, hotel rooms, and, as rumor has it, even entertainment of the 'flesh.' "

That first World Series was the beginning of the end of baseball as a national sport. After that it became mass entertainment. Who watches the Series in the Yankee Stadium today? A few fans, to be sure, as well as many who never saw a baseball game before. Others are those peculiar celebrities who attend every big sporting event, plus out-of-town buyers who are able to arrange to be in Manhattan the first week of October, and happen to be good friends of Joe.

At present tickets for the Series are sold in packets of three, costing $8.80 apiece. That is, you must pay $26.40 and buy seats for three games. Most fans cannot afford this. The managements, who usually look on baseball as you do croquet, spend their energies in profitable real-estate deals and arguing over the oil rights underneath second base. The chief differences between the modern magnates and the earlier ones was shown that fall of 1903 by Barney Dreyfuss. According to their contracts, the Pittsburgh players were obliged to play in the first Series without extra compensation. Dreyfuss not only paid them extra, but turned over his share of the profits to be divided among the team.

The modern fan would also notice that the crowd included no women—but many youngsters. Nowadays a boy of twelve who sees the Series watches it by television, unless Daddy happens to be a vice-president of General Gumbat, Inc. You would also observe that the players tossing the ball back and forth below wore no numbers. None were necessary. The spectators not only knew every man by sight, they were seated close enough to the field to distinguish their faces.

When we took our seats, the Pirates were already working out on the diamond. That giant with the jutting jaw around second is Honus Wagner.

John Peter Wagner, who played short for the Pirates twenty-one years, was a gorilla-like man with long arms and legs. He was discovered by Ed Barrow, later president of the Yankees, for whom he played in one of the first night games, at

*Two of baseball's immortals, Cy Young of Boston (l) and Honus
Wagner of Pittsburgh—both played in first World Series;
Young sold tickets, pitched, and won final game.*

Wilmington, Delaware, on July 4, 1896. Wagner led the National League for eight years with a lifetime batting average of .389, hitting against a pellet like a ping-pong ball, and was one of the eight men in the major leagues who ever made more than three thousand hits. (The others are Cap Anson, Nap Lajoie, Ty Cobb, Tris Speaker, Eddie Collins, Paul Waner, and Stan Musial.) Not until he had won his fifth straight batting title in succession was his salary raised to $10,000. Ted Williams signed in 1958 with the Boston Red Sox for $135,000. Baseball has come a long ways since 1903.

On first for Pittsburgh was "Kitty" Bransfield, and shagging flies in left was Fred Clarke, the Pitt captain, and the first ballplayer ever to wear sunglasses. The uniforms of the umpires would be familiar. Also the dimensions of the diamond, ninety feet from base to base. But not that rope stretched in an arc from left to right, with fans standing ten deep behind. The playing area of this new ball park was a vast expanse some five hundred feet from home plate to the fence in center field, about fifty feet more than the average park today. At four hundred and fifty feet, the rope had been stretched from one foul line to the other. Hits into the crowd went for three, not two, bases.

Gradually the Pilgrims appeared in white. (It was several years before we boys realized other teams than Boston wore white uniforms at home.) There was Cy Freeman, the right fielder, who led the American League that year in homers (thirteen), triples (twenty-one), and doubles (thirty-nine). Soon George La-Chance, the first baseman, and Pat Dougherty, the left fielder and leading hitter on the club, appeared.

Pitchers were indeed iron men in the early days of baseball, and pitching dominated the first Series. Only one reliever was used by either side in the eight games, as against twenty-one in the 1955 Series when the Dodgers beat the Yankees. In 1903 the burden was carried by four men: Sam Leever, the top man in the National League, with a 25 to 7 record that summer, Phillippi, 25 to 8, for Pittsburgh, "Big Bill" Dineen, 21 to 11, and Young, 29 to 9, for Boston. The two Pirate hurlers, who had won the pennant between them, established a record that season of six straight shutouts and fifty-one scoreless innings in succession. It has never been equaled.

Phillippi, the workhorse of their staff, was six-feet two-inches tall and weighed one hundred and eighty pounds. He pitched in five of the eight Series games. The last afternoon he was going with only forty-eight hours' rest. Whereas Dineen for Boston was fresh. The crisis of the game came in the fourth when Tommy Leach singled and Honus Wagner came to bat as the band played "Down Where the Wurzburger Flows."

Honus responded like a money player by singling to right. Bransfield popped up, and then Claude Ritchey beat out an infield hit, filling the bases with one away. With Sebring at bat for Pittsburgh, Lou Criger the Boston catcher called for a pitchout. He took the ball, stepped forward to throw to second, turned and whipped the ball to Collins on third, catching Leach off the bag. The rally died when

Phelps, the next batter, grounded to Freddy Parent, the Boston shortstop, and the Loyal Rooters were ecstatic.

This proved to be Pittsburgh's last chance. In between innings Cy Young, who was warming up back of the grandstand with Duke Farrell, wormed his way through the crowd to see whether Dineen needed help. But Big Bill had the visitors under control. In Boston's half, Candy LaChance tripled with a man aboard, and scored on a deep fly. The Pilgrims picked up another run in the sixth to lead 3 to 0.

In the seventh, tempers ran high. First, Collins came in from third to scoop up a bunt with his bare hand and throw out the runner, a new play at the time. Then Fred Clarke, who felt Dineen was throwing at his head, bunted down the first-base line, intending to spike him. This was a trick for which he was celebrated.

But LaChance was ready. He raced in, let the ball roll past, and as Clarke went by picked it up and threw hard at his back. Players instantly swarmed from the benches onto the diamond, fans broke through the ropes, and soon a mob ten feet deep surrounded the diamond. It was half an hour before the umpires, Hank O'Day of the National League and Tommy Connolly of the American, could force the fans behind the ropes in center field and resume the game.

When Dineen struck out Wagner at the end, the fans tumbled onto the field. They cheered, shrieked, hoisted up the players, and paraded round and round the field behind their band, followed by the Loyal Rooters. It was more than an hour before the defeated Pirates could get through to their carriages waiting out on Huntington Avenue.

Fans who tried to hoist players to their shoulders after a Series game today would be arrested at once for assault and battery. Nor is it likely you'll ever see Mickey Mantle selling tickets on the morning of the last game outside the Yankee Stadium in New York.

MAN WHO JUMPS WITH THE DEVIL

by John Lovesey

A first-hand account of the only "perfect" jump ever scored, written for Sports Illustrated
in 1964 by a free lance journalist whose beat is the world.

IN THE DANGEROUS AND DEMANDING WORLD of international ski jumping, each
competitor finds his mind riveted on two distant goals. One, obviously, is to jump
farther than anyone else. This he may do. The other is to make the perfect jump,
to attain that unwavering symmetry of style which will receive the maximum
score from the five judges. This, by all the power of logic and the traditions of the
sport, he may not do. For no man can be expected to achieve perfection while
hurtling off an icy platform at 60 mph to land some 100 yards away, subject en
route to all the vagaries of wind, fog, his own fear and the normal prejudices of
the presiding judges. And, indeed, no man ever had achieved perfection until
one year ago when Norway's Toralf Engan executed a leap of such artistry and
power that the astounded judges gave him the highest score recorded in modern
jumping history. Everyone conceded this was, indeed, the ultimate.

In his search for perfection, Engan had to overcome a crippling case of nerves
while toughening his muscles until both mind and body became as hard as his
hickory skis. Along the way he won an unprecedented string of championships
and restored to his country the pre-eminence in jumping which had been lost to
the Finns 10 years ago. Now, because of his flawless skill, because of the fierce
concentration born of a score of years pursuing that perfect jump, Toralf Engan
is an overwhelming favorite to win both the special jumping events at the Innsbruck Olympics.

In 1962 Engan took the almost impossible total of 24 out of 27 meets, including the world championship at Zakopane, Poland. Last year he compiled 17
victories, including an all-important triumph over East Germany's 1960 Olympic
champion, Helmut Recknagel, on Innsbruck's Bergisel Hill, where the gold
medal will be contested.

Because of Engan, Norwegians feel a renewed burst of national pride. There
are 10,000 ski jumps of all sizes in Norway and all in good use. "Every time a
small boy sets out for a small jump, he is a small Engan," says one Norwegian.
Girls smother their bedroom walls with his pictures. Anything Engan does be-
comes news. His biography, *On the Top,* became a bestseller. Crowds turn out to

watch him practice on the world-famous Holmenkollen jump at Oslo, even in the freezing night that makes the city glitter like an open jewel box.

Norway's national hero is 27 years old, a solid, 5-foot 6-inch, 143-pound package of tightly controlled emotion. He was born and lives in Holonda, a small, pleasant, remote rural village near Trondheim. Engan works in Trondheim for a sports equipment dealer and is informally engaged to a blonde clothing-store clerk named Elin Halvorsen. "I will marry," he says, "when I have the time."

Toralf began to ski in the woods around home at three. By seven he was jumping on skis left by the German army of occupation. When his father hit it lucky in a lottery, he bought Toralf his second pair of skis, and at 13 Toralf won the county championship. In 1955 he went off the big Holmenkollen Hill and won the national junior championship. By all outward indications, he should have then leaped right on to bigger prizes. But Norway's vast army of jumping experts, including the coaches in Engan's own ski club, dismissed him as a future champion because of his painfully obvious nerves. Jumpers have a deep devil inside that drives them to a kind of ice-cold fury before a start. Engan had this devil, but he was unable to control it. Before every meet he threw up his breakfast. His concentration was poor, his mind so tense and preoccupied that his jumps were sloppy. Furthermore, under the often haphazard training provided by his ski club coaches, Engan simply was not physically strong enough.

"When I was with the group," he explains, "and followed the basic training program, I found that after some events I felt weak. I told the trainers that I wanted to coach myself and try my own methods."

For two years Engan stopped jumping and put himself on a punishing program of muscle-building that he still follows. In the summer he plays soccer and dives from a springboard. All year round, four or five times a week, he does deep knee bends with a 100-pound weight across his shoulders. With a 30-pound sack of sand on his back, he hops on alternate feet up stadium steps, then jumps, feet together, over 3-foot-7-inch-high hurdles. His legs became so powerful that now, from a standing position, he can broad-jump 9 feet and high-jump 4½ feet. "Unlike most Norwegians," says a countryman, "Toralf has discipline."

As he whipped his body into shape Engan also polished his jumping technique, adopting the winning style of the Finns. From the top of a big hill like the Bergisel or the Holmenkollen, the inrun drops some 280 feet, a narrow, 42-degree pitch of crusty snow that has been watered and packed into sheer glaze ice. Engan began to master the frightening business of the quick push-step onto the inrun, the tight crouch with body curled against his knees as he gathered speed for the mile-a-minute takeoff. As he flashed off the lip, he learned to throw his body far forward, his back slightly bent in the shape of an airplane wing section. As he hurtled outward, Engan's nose came to within mere inches of his ski tips, his arms at his sides so his hands could guide his flight like the ailerons of a plane. Just as important, he began to get real power in his takeoff. Today his extreme push off the lip is so strong that he may at any time overjump the

The perfect jump.

steep landing slope on any hill, and to protect himself he frequently has to step onto the inrun farther down than the normal starting point.

In the discipline of physical training Engan also developed the mental muscle to hold his nerves in check. He has learned to withdraw into himself completely before a meet. In the last hours before a jump he spends 30 minutes silently waxing his skis. Then he inspects his boots and bindings, and meticulously goes over the jump in his mind. "I am criticized," he says, "because I don't talk to others before jumping, but I am using these things to help me concentrate. I try to control my body right down to my feet. I have been teaching myself this since I was 15."

By 1959, though Engan had trained hard enough to be considered one of the top half a dozen jumpers in Norway, he still was not up to Olympic standards.

Photograph by Ivan Aaserud, Oslo, Norway

After the tryouts for the 1960 team that went to Squaw Valley he was left off the squad. At the time it was reported that he was sick and unable to travel. However, Thorleif Schjelderup, once Engan's coach, emphatically believes it was still nerves, not physical sickness, that kept Engan off the 1960 Olympic team. But Engan himself demurs. "When we competed I just wasn't good enough."

Within a year, however, his Spartan program of mind and muscle training took hold, and Engan was, suddenly, good enough for anybody. In 1961 he won five of ten meets, and in late March of 1962, after 22 more victories, he soared off the Holmenkollen Hill to win the oldest and, Olympics aside, most prestigious prize in winter sport. Still, Engan was dissatisfied. In his mind, always dangling just out of reach, he saw the image of the perfect jump. Before a meet in Falun, Sweden, only a year ago, he said, "Every time I jump there is a failure. On some jumps the only thing I have done wrong is move a hand. When I make the good jump I am like an airplane, gliding with everything under control, completely safe, and with not a note of fear. But on the day when I make the perfect jump I will spring like a gazelle, float through the air and land as light as a feather."

Then, amazingly, at Falun he made it, the perfect jump shown at left, sailing 272 feet to break the hill record. He achieved a flight of sheer beauty, his arms pinned to his sides, his landing as elegant as a dancer's.

Even with the perfect jump behind him, however, Engan will still admit to fears sharp enough to occasionally penetrate his wall of will. "There are only two things that I am afraid of on the hill," he says. "One is fog. Sometimes I can see only 30 feet in front of me and 20 down the slope. It must be the same feeling a flyer feels when he is piloting a plane through a thick cloud. I have to calculate all the way and hope for the best."

The other fear is wind. "Very often up in the hills it blows hard. This is more dangerous than fog, and you have to maneuver with your hands to keep in line with the hill. You can steer like an aircraft, waving the hands and moving the skis up and down." Jumpers often have a distinct, but false, impression that they are going to land in the crowd.

Curiously, for a man who compares his jumps to airplanes and who has come closer to flying than most men since Icarus, Engan is afraid of traveling by plane. He goes to extraordinary lengths to drive to competitions in his black Volkswagen. But even driving on the road can fill him with subliminal dread.

"Sometimes when I have been pumped out by a competition and have driven hundreds of miles home, I dream. I am driving my car too fast. Just as I am about to crash, I wake in a cold sweat, sitting up gripping the bottom of my bed. Then I laugh. I am safe."

In Engan's tightrope style, a jumping theory translated into astonishing reality, one slip means failure. In the 1963 Norwegian national championships, a few weeks after his perfect jump, he did slip, his fourth fall in 400 jumps. His tremendous spring carried him four yards beyond the hill record of 263 feet for a jarring landing on unprepared snow. Shortly thereafter, weakened by an attack of flu, and just possibly by a last, lingering case of nerves ("At the top of the jump, I listen to the whole crowd, knowing that they are expecting everything of me"), he fell again in an attempt to win his second successive Holmenkollen title. Norway was astounded, but not downcast, since the winner was Engan's countryman, Torbjorn Yggeseth. But Norway—in fact, the whole ski-jumping world—was even more astounded by the second and fourth finishers in the 1963 Holmenkollen: John Balfanz of Minneapolis, and Gene Kotlarek of Duluth.

Balfanz was the first American ever to place in a major European jump. Kotlarek was only a fraction of a point out of third. And they achieved these unprecedented results with such authority and poise that they must—along with Yggeseth, Recknagel, Veikko Kankkonen of Finland, and perhaps one of the fast-improving Russians—be considered the main threats to Engan on the Bergisel Hill.

Engan, however, is unconcerned with any single rival, regardless of nationality. His one thought is to prove, finally, that he is the world's premier jumper, and he is convinced that he will succeed. Indeed, he contemplates the Olympic competition with obvious delight. "I feel more supple," he says, "and stronger in the legs. My bad form at the end of last season has turned me into an attacker rather than the defender. I have to mount the throne again. This goads me to extra effort."

To insure the success of that effort, he returned last spring and summer to his relentless training schedule. He also honed his balance by springboard diving and walking a tightwire. Then, when the early snow fell in the mountains around Trondheim, he was the first man out with skis. "It was good to feel snow under them," he says. "But I did not jump before December. My training program was more important." During the past few weeks, however, he has been jumping with all his former zest and precision. In his mind, too, he is confident and at ease.

"I honestly feel more relaxed, as if I have come of age," he says. "I want to be back in the position I was before Holmenkollen and I think my frame of mind today gives me the necessary inner strength to do it. I'm more optimistic than ever before."

"If Engan succeeds on a hill," Coach Schjelderup says, "the others are just competing there for second place. Only his nerves can beat him."

Engan feels now that nothing can beat him. "I have locked my mind and I have conquered my nerves," he says. "Only after the last jump of a competition I turn a lock to unfree my mind. Again, I became an ordinary man."

THE COURAGEOUS ONE

by Carl T. Rowan

It took two to crumble the baseball color wall. The how of it was told in a book published in 1960 by the former Director of the U.S. Office of Information.

Branch Rickey knew that it was time for him to talk directly to Robinson, and to make his personal, man-to-man assessment of Robinson's qualifications to lead a revolution that Rickey felt would be crucial in both their lives. He sat in his office one day in early August, 1945, thinking about the way in which this issue had divided his family. His son, Branch, Jr., was completely in favor of the Dodgers' bringing a Negro into organized baseball, but he feared other owners would make life miserable for his father. Mrs. Rickey, Sr., also feared reaction.

"Branch," she had pleaded, "you're too old to go through this ordeal, too old to take the abuse they'll heap on you."

"A man is never too old to do what he knows is right and what his conscience tells him he must do," Rickey replied.

Then there were the daughters. "Lord," Rickey said to his wife, "that Jane"—a daughter in Elmira, N.Y.—"how she's supporting me. What a leaning post she has become, because she believes I ought to do it on the basis of principle. And Alice—she's got her oar in the water and she's pulling for me to beat the band. Mary and Sue—they're neutral, but I think they know that I've got to do this thing because it's right."

In late August, Rickey called in his most trusted aide, Sukeforth, and asked him to find Robinson and bring him to Brooklyn if he was convinced on this final viewing that the Negro really could make good as a baseball player. Sukeforth had trouble locating the Monarchs, who were playing a notoriously unreliable schedule, as Negro teams usually did, but finally he caught them at Comiskey Park in Chicago. Someone told him that Robinson would be wearing Number 8. Sukeforth bought a box seat ticket and waited. Finally he saw Number 8, the husky, muscular, pigeon-toed player who kept chattering in a high-pitched voice as he pounded his fist into his glove. Sukeforth stepped to

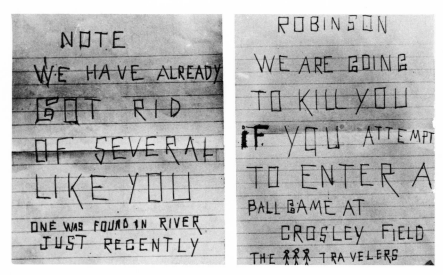

". . . guts enough not to fight back."

the railing and motioned to Robinson, who walked over with a clearly suspicious look on his face.

"You're Jackie Robinson, right?"

"That's right."

"I'm Clyde Sukeforth of the Brooklyn Dodger organization."

Robinson gave a look of disbelief.

"Seriously, I represent the Brooklyn Dodgers. You might have heard that Branch Rickey, our general manager, is organizing another Negro league and a team of Brown Dodgers. He's eager to get some topnotch ball players. We've heard a lot of glowing reports about you and he asked me to come out tonight and look you over. He wants me to see you throw a few from the hole at shortstop."

Robinson thought of the runaround in Boston, but he was convinced that Sukeforth really represented the Dodgers. He had heard rumors of the Brown Dodgers.

"You won't see me throw any from the hole tonight," Robinson said. "I've got a bum shoulder. Fell on it a couple of days ago, and the trainer says I'll be out for a week."

"I see," said Sukeforth. "But I sure would like to talk to you after the game. Any chance of your meeting me?"

Robinson was silent as he pounded the pocket of his glove a couple times more with his fist. "What did you say your name was?"

Sukeforth spelled it out for him and told Robinson that he was staying at the Stevens, where he would be waiting in the lobby near the cigar stand.

"Sure, I'll drop by to talk to you. Ought to get there before midnight."

Waiting for Robinson, Sukeforth sat in the cocktail lounge, mulling over the instructions Rickey had given him. Rickey was still concerned about Robinson's ability to go to his right from the shortstop position and make that long throw to first. Sukeforth was unsure what to do, since he could not see Robinson play. Yet the boss seemed to want very much to talk to this player, so Sukeforth decided to ask Robinson to go to Brooklyn with him.

On the morning of August 28, 1945, Sukeforth led a bewildered young ballplayer into the office of a man who had an awesome reputation even among experienced players who had never been burdened by insecurities imposed by race. That morning, during three extraordinary hours in the walnut-paneled office of perhaps the smartest baseball man of his time, the mark of history was stamped on twenty-six-year-old Jackie Robinson.

As he and Sukeforth strode into this finely furnished office, decorated with a lighted fish tank, the man with the round belly and bushy brows got out of his leather swivel chair, shifted his cigar from the pudgy fingers on his right

". . . fidelity to your race, and to this crucial cause that you symbolize."

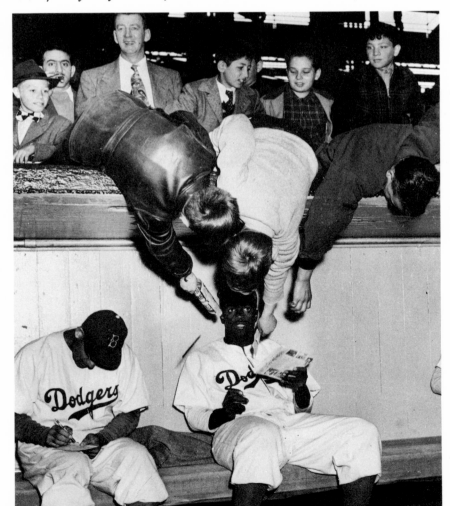

hand to those of his left and shook hands with Robinson. The formal pleasantries were brief, for Rickey quickly asked Jackie: "You got a girl?"

Embarrassed to face such a personal question so soon, Jackie replied hesitantly, "I don't know."

"What do you mean, you don't know?"

"I mean that I had a girl, one to whom I'm engaged, but the way I've been traveling around with the Monarchs, never seeing her or anything, a fellow can't be sure if he's got a girl or not."

"Is she a fine girl, good family background, educated girl?"

"They don't come finer, Mr. Rickey."

"Then you know doggone well you've got a girl! When we get through today you may want to call her up, 'cause there are times when a man needs a woman by his side. By the way, are you under contract to the Monarchs?"

"No, sir."

"Do you have any agreement with them, written or oral, to play with them either the rest of this year, next year or any length of time?"

"No, sir. No agreement whatsoever except that they pay me a certain amount every payday. But we just play from payday to payday. Either one of us could break it off at the end of the month if necessary."

"Tell me, Jackie, do you have any idea why I want to talk to you?"

"All I know is what Mr. Sukeforth told me, and the rumors I've been hearing about you starting a new Negro league and a team called the Brown Dodgers."

"No, Jackie, that isn't really it. You were brought here to play for the Brooklyn organization—perhaps, as a start, for Montreal."

Robinson was stunned. Was this another in that long string of situations in which he, like other Negroes, was encouraged to build mountains of hopes and dreams, only to see them tumble at the last minute?

"Me? Me play with Montreal . . . ?"

"If you can make it. If you make the grade."

Rickey turned to Sukeforth and asked him whether he thought Robinson could make the grade.

"He's a good ballplayer, Mr. Rickey," Sukeforth replied. "Probably the best bunter you ever laid eyes on, and can he run those bases!"

Rickey's voice rose into a stentorian roar. This man, who was an orator even if only asking someone to pass the salt and pepper, flailed his arms and cried out: "I know he's a ballplayer. I've watched him. We scouted you for weeks, Jackie. We know what you can do on the baseball field. But this means more than being able to play baseball. I mean, have you got the guts?"

"I'll make it if I get the opportunity . . ." said Robinson in a comparative whisper.

Now Rickey was thundering again. "I want to be honest with you, Jackie. I want to level with you here today. I heard all the stories of racial resentment toward you. They told me out in Pasadena that you're a racial agitator. They told me at UCLA that in basketball you had trouble with coaches, players and officials. I just want to tell you that my thorough investigation convinced me that the criticisms are unjustified, that if you'd been white it would have been nothing. So I'm dismissing these rumors as not amounting to a hill of beans. But the thing I want to convince you of," he fairly bellowed as he pounded his desk, "is that we can't fight our way through this. Jackie, we've got no army . . ." and his voice was trailing off into a murmur ". . . there's virtually nobody on our side. No owners, no umpires, very few newspapermen. And I'm afraid that many fans may be hostile. We'll be in a tough position, Jackie. We can win only if we can convince the world that I'm doing this because you're a great ballplayer, a fine gentleman.

"So there's more than just playing," Rickey continued, his voice rising rapidly again. "I wish it meant only hits, runs and errors—only the things they put in the box score. Because you know—yes, *you* would know, Jackie—that a baseball box score is a democratic thing. It doesn't tell how big you are, what church you attend, what color you are or how your father voted in the last election. It just tells what kind of baseball player you were on that particular day."

"Mr. Rickey, when the chips are down, isn't what they put in the box score what really counts?" said Jackie, warming up to the man now, realizing that Rickey's loud bark was a lot worse than his bite, feeling that there was something he too could contribute to this startling discussion.

"Yes, it's all that *ought* to count, but it isn't. Maybe one of these days it *will* be all that counts. That's one of the reasons why I've got you here, Jackie. If you're a good enough ballplayer, and a big enough man, we can make this a start in the right direction. But let me tell you it's going to take an awful lot of courage."

Rickey strode over and put his face close to Robinson's, which was now gleaming with tiny beads of perspiration; there were wrinkles etched deeply in his forehead, a sign of intense concentration. "Have you got the guts to play the game no matter what happens? That's what I want to know!" Rickey exclaimed.

"I think I can play the game, Mr. Rickey," said Robinson without flinching.

"All right. You're standing in the batter's box in a tense situation. I'm a notorious bean-baller. I wing a fast one at you that grazes your cap and sends you sprawling back on your butt. What do you do?"

"It won't be the first time a pitcher threw one at me, Mr. Rickey," Robinson said matter-of-factly.

Rickey leaned back and studied Robinson's features for a few seconds. "All right," he said. "All right. So I'm an opposing player, and we're in the heat of a crucial game. I slap the ball out into the field and I'm rounding first and I charge into second and we have a close play and I collide with you. As we untangle I lunge toward you"—he lunged toward Robinson—"and I shout, 'Get out of my way, you dirty black son of a bitch!' What do you do?"

Robinson was silent, remembering those days in Pasadena when anyone who hurled that kind of epithet at him, in a football game or out of one, was likely to get his nose punched in. He looked at Rickey, waiting for the answer, and he licked his lips and swallowed. He knew the answer Rickey wanted. That he would grin and bear it. But before he could get the answer out, Rickey was unfolding another situation. "You're playing shortstop and I come down from first, stealing, flying in with my spikes high, and I cut you in the leg. As the blood trickles down your shin I grin at you and say, 'Now how do you like that, nigger boy?' What do you do?"

Robinson was burning hot inside. Here stood a black man with a tremendous self-respect born out of adversity, a man with a burning sense of pride. His whole life had been an effort to convince the white people around him that even though the Negro was outnumbered, even though he might be fettered by new shackles imposed by society, even though he carried the burdens of poor education, poor economic background—that no matter what had ever been said, the Negro was not a coward—not a coward against any odds. "Mr. Rickey," he said, "do you want a ballplayer who's afraid to fight back?"

Rickey's face wrinkled in mock rage as he shouted, "I want a ballplayer with guts enough not to fight back!"

Rickey turned his back on Robinson and walked across the floor. Momentarily he was back again in front of Jackie, his hands out and his palms skyward as if pleading with the young Negro. "Remember what I said, Jackie. This is one battle we can't *fight* our way through. Remember what I said, Jackie: no army, no owners, no umpires, virtually nobody on our side. This is a battle in which you'll have to swallow an awful lot of pride and count on base hits and stolen bases to do the job. That's what'll do it, Jackie. Nothing else."

But Branch Rickey was not through. He was removing his jacket and rolling up his sleeves so he could act out all the hostile personalities that baseball's first Negro was likely to face. He posed as a hotel clerk telling Robinson that "no niggers can sleep here"; as a restaurant manager telling Robinson that he couldn't eat out front with the rest of the team, but that they would prepare sandwiches for him to eat in the bus, or fix him a meal in the kitchen; as an umpire calling Robinson out on a bum decision and then barking out angry words reflecting on the color of Robinson's face.

Now, his shirt wet at the collarbone and under the armpits, his face gleaming with perspiration, Rickey had projected Robinson from the Montreal Royals to the Brooklyn Dodgers and into the World Series. "So we play for keeps, there, Jackie; we play it there to win, and almost everything under the sun goes. I want to win in the most desperate way, so I'm coming into second with my spikes flying. But you don't give ground. You're tricky. You feint, and as I hurl myself you ease out of the way and jam that ball hard into my ribs. As I lie there in the swirling dust, my rib aching, I hear that umpire crying, 'You're out,' and I jump up, and all I can see is that black face of yours shining in front of my eyes. So

I yell, 'Don't hit me with a ball like that, you tarbaby son of a bitch.' So I haul off and I sock you right in the cheek." Rickey waved his massive fist in Robinson's face, missing it only by a whisper. Robinson's nose twitched and his lips moved a bit. But his head was steady.

"I get it, Mr. Rickey, I get it," the Negro said. "What you want me to say is that I've got another cheek."

Rickey smiled with satisfaction. He pulled out a white handkerchief and wiped the sweat off his face. Then he strode back to his desk and pulled out a copy of Papini's *Life of Christ*.

Rickey began to read from the philosophy of Papini, who went into seclusion to write a derogatory report on the life of Christ and ended up by writing a laudation. Then Rickey handed the book to Jackie. "Read these passages of Papini's philosophy," he ordered. Robinson took the book and began to read silently:

NONRESISTANCE

But Jesus has not yet arrived at the most stupefying of His revolutionary teachings. "Ye have heard that it hath been said, An eye for an eye, and a tooth for a tooth: But I say unto you, That ye resist not evil: But whosoever shall smite thee on thy right cheek, turn to him the other also. And if any man will sue thee at the law, and take away thy coat, let him have thy cloak also. And whosoever shall compel thee to go a mile, go with him twain."

There could be no more definite repudiation of the old law of retaliation. The greater part of those who call themselves Christians not only have never observed this new Commandment, but have never been willing to pretend to approve of it. For an infinite number of believers this principle of not resisting evil has been the unendurable and inacceptable scandal of Christianity . . .

When Robinson handed the book back to Rickey the old baseball wizard was smiling. He offered a few more sentences to Robinson as what he later called "the glue to hold his resolution firm": "Jackie, I just want to beg two things of you: that as a baseball player you give it your utmost; and as a man you give continuing fidelity to your race and to this crucial cause that you symbolize."

When this almost unbelievable three hours was over, Branch Rickey held no doubt that Jackie Robinson was the man he wanted. Robinson agreed to accept a bonus of $3,500 and a salary of $600 a month as part of what was, in effect, a contract to play baseball with the Montreal Royals.

Rickey explained to Robinson the need to keep their agreement secret because he did not want to announce it publicly until December.

Jackie telephoned his mother and Rachel to tell them about this fantastic development, and went back to his job with the Monarchs.

LARSEN PITCHES
FIRST SERIES NO-HITTER

by Dan Parker

A long-time columnist for the New York Daily Mirror *wrote of the "impossible" which occurred during the World Series of 1956.*

THERE'S A LAMP POST in the publicity-conscious city of St. Petersburg, Fla., which, if I know my Al Lang, will shortly bear a bronze plaque lettered in bold relief as follows:

"Don Larsen crashed into this post at 6 a.m., Tuesday, April 3d, 1956, while training with the New York Yankees to pitch the first perfect World Series game in history."

Among the 64,519 who saw Don, the Playboy of the Western World, accomplish the miraculous feat that has been the goal of many pitchers who have preceded him in this, the 286th Series game, was Mr. Lang, St. Petersburg's elderly but ageless good will ambassador. So if the bronze plaque isn't riveted to the lamp post that should become St. Pete's most famous landmark in time for the approaching annual influx of winter residents, Al will be to blame.

Remarkable from any angle viewed, Larsen's classic takes on added lustre from the fact that the big right-hander came to the Yankees two years ago this winter in the deal with Baltimore—like the potato the Louisiana bayou country storekeeper sticks on the spout of his customer's kerosene can to keep it from spilling.

This classic that the Yankees' problem child unfolded before a tense crowd in the fifth game of the Series, putting them out in front 3 to 2, as the caravan moves back to Ebbets Field for a fight to the death, exploded all the homilies ever written about the rewards of clean living and, in the process, toppled a recently crowned idol from his pedestal. It was Sal Maglie, still basking in the adulation of American fandom after his remarkable performances for the Dodgers this season, who felt the full force of Larsen's inconoclasm. With cool contempt for the Dodger ace, who had instilled fear in his not easily scared teammates in the opening game of the Series, Larsen set about his job as if bent on settling for not just a no-hitter, but a perfect one. And, as the afternoon wore on, and the products of Larsen's limb grew more lethal, the feeling grew that he was going to make it, where all the others had failed.

. . . a potato stuck on the spout of a kerosene can.

Inwardly, the usually happy-go-lucky roisterer who thinks training rules were made to be broken, was rankling because Casey Stengel had removed him in the second inning of the second game with the Yanks leading, 6-1, the bases loaded and two out. Larsen thought he should have been left in and developments, in the form of a deluge of runs that redeemed a seemingly lost cause for the Dodgers, supported his contention.

This time, big Don's slogan was: "I shall not pass!" His control was perfection personified. The nearest he came to putting a batter on base was when Peewee Reese, second man up, worked him to a three and two count before letting a third strike whizz by, unmolested. But it took three fielding gems, one of them on the freakish side, to keep Larsen's sanctum inviolate. He almost lost his Hall of Fame clincher when Jackie Robinson opened the second by lining a hot cannon ball at Andy Carey, who stuck up a glove in self defense. The ball deflected foul to Gil McDougall, who saved the day for Larsen with a peg that nailed Jackie at first by the thinnest of eyelashes. You'll see this kind of play once in a blue moon—usually on the day when a perfect ball game is in the making.

The nearest thing to a base hit, however, if we overlook two skin-of-your-teeth foul homers by Snider in the 4th, and Amoros in the 5th into the right field stands, was Gil Hodges' drive to deep left center in the fifth. This smash seemed ticketed for extra bases as Mickey Mantle, supposedly unable to cut loose with the Doberman-Pinschers, outraced the ball to pull it in with his gloved hand just at the last split second. Besides being a life-saver for Larsen, this fielding gem of purest ray serene was Snider's come-uppance for perpetrating diving grand larceny on Yogi Berra in the fourth by committing merely the impossible in gathering in his sinking liner a fraction of an inch above the blades of grass.

The final saver for Larsen was the product of a bit of lightning glove work by Carey in the eighth when he stabbed Hodges' projectile with his glove, and as it glanced upward off the leather, grabbed it on the way down. Just to make sure, he threw to first but Gil, who by this time figured he just couldn't win, had stopped running. He didn't need the exercise and, besides, had made the team long ago.

As Furillo, 25th man to face Larsen, opened the ninth by lifting an easy fly to Hank Bauer, the crowd, almost ready to explode from tension, started the cheer. When Campanella grounded to Martin for the second out, it seemed as if hearts stopped beating everywhere in the park as the fate of Floyd Bevens, the last Yankee pitcher to reach this stage of the game without yielding a hit to the Dodgers in a Series game (1947), came to mind. Out of the dugout, swinging a bat, stepped, not Sal Maglie, Wednesday's hero, whose turn it was, but Dale Mitchell, the ex-Cleveland Indian's spray hitter whose left-hand batting style made him Brooklyn's last hope.

Larsen, grabbing the rosin bag, rubbing his pants and looking as close to being fidgety as he had been at any time during the game, served him a ball. Next, he shot over a strike that Mitchell disdained. Again Donnybrook—correction, Donny Boy—fired one down the slot and Mitchell swiped at it without touching leather. One pitch away from the realization of a dream that has always seemed as impossible of fulfillment as one of a pitcher striking out every batter on three pitches, Larsen looked at Yogi for the sign, and let Mitchell have his fast ball. Dale looked, hesitated, and let it go by—thereby putting the finishing touches on Larson's all-time masterpiece.

Afterwards, in the club house, Dale said: "It was outside." What he probably meant was "outside the realm of possibility," which was what everyone else thought Don's feat was, until they saw it performed.

Get busy on that plaque, St. Petersburg, before Don knocks down a pole in some other town, celebrating his miracle . . . with the complete permission of one Charles Dillon Stengel, a most understanding manager.

THE
LOSERS

KILL THE BIG BUM

by H. C. Witwer

An all but forgotten name of yesterday, yet incontestably one of the big writers of any day, as this razor-slash at the manly art, written in 1921, will confirm.

As a result of the wide publicity given the million-dollar purses which certain promoters are beseeching Messrs. Dempsey and Carpentier to accept for what will be a possible five-minute exhibition of assault and battery, prize fighting has driven the cleaner and healthier sports momentarily out of the limelight. It is, perhaps, not to be wondered that many a strapping young collegian, poring over his studies, sighs reflectively and allows a tentative hand to stray to his biceps. As opposed to the inevitable grind at meager pay before success comes at law, medicine, business, any of the arts or sciences, the prospect of getting half a million dollars within a couple of years for a few minutes' exhibition of the "manly art" is extremely alluring. That the vast majority of professional bruisers batter or get battered into disfiguring insensibility week after week for a few dollars, that the average paid boxer is "through" long before thirty-five, and that most of them, even ex-champions, die destitute and forgotten, is seldom, if ever, stressed by the prize-fight enthusiast.

According to its admirers, prize fighting develops physical and moral courage to the highest degree, even implants self-respect, good sportsmanship, and a sense of fair play where those elements have been lacking, and, in a word, is at all times a most edifying and character-building spectacle.

A notable example of the latter was furnished last July at Toledo, when Dempsey pounded the blood-covered and half-conscious wreck of Willard from one side of the ring to the other, to the accompaniment of a chorus of such typically sportsmanlike expressions as "Kill the big bum!" As to the physical and moral courage inculcated by the prize ring, I have seen punishment assimilated in an inter-collegiate football game that would make the average prize fighter jump out of the ring. For the moral courage, glance at the war record of the pugilists as a class. The majority of our own "fighters" went on the "See America First!" principle, and many from other countries, particularly England, slipped over here and stayed bomb-proof during the recent unpleasantness. Naturally, there were individual exceptions. A few American boxers saw service in France, and Carpentier himself won honors as an aviator, but I am sure that was *in spite* of the fact that those men were professional maulers and not *because* of it. Again, a perusal of the professions of those who were commended for extraordinary bravery in action will show clerks, bookkeepers, salesmen, farmers, etc.—few, if any, prize fighters. Our most decorated doughboy, Sergeant York, was a minister.

The American Legion is very much exercised at present over the proposed Dempsey-Carpentier bout. Action is being taken to prevent the holding of the contest in the United States on the ground that Dempsey, the war-time ship-builder, should not be permitted to represent America as its "greatest fighter." Without going into the merits of this viewpoint, when one thinks that Dempsey, who never got nearer France than the Newark (N.J.) Bay Shipyards, may get three or four hundred thousand dollars for fighting *one* man a few minutes with a pair of six-ounce gloves and that the average doughboy got thirty-three dollars a month for fighting a couple of million men for a year with a bayonet, it is not hard to sympathize with those indignant ex-members of the A. E. F.— thousands of whom are jobless and recovering from grievous wounds.

The impression of one who by some years of actual experience has accumulated a little first-hand knowledge of the sordid atmosphere surrounding modern professional pugilism (not amateur boxing—an admirable exercise and a vastly different sport) is that it is a great thing to keep away from. It is no more conducted with the idea of improving the breed of the genus *homo* than present-day horse racing is devoted to the improvement of the breed of the horse. To the young, clean, husky youth who is regarding a career in the prize ring with a contemplative eye, I would suggest a ringside seat, not at a championship battle, but at some of the bouts between second and third-raters, where he would naturally begin his own apprenticeship. Let him observe the contestants and their "handlers," listen to the supervile admonitions or expletives hurled at a battered loser by the crowd, absorb some of the general atmosphere—and then make his choice!

A few of our well-known colleges have added box fightin' to their regular courses for the young and ambitious as a result of the inmates gnashin' their teeth and swoonin' away on the dear old campus when they heard of a million-dollar purse for the heavyweight championship of the world. It's commencin' to look kinda silly to the little pals of Alma Mater for them to toy with readin' and 'ritin' and 'rithmetic for a four-year hitch, and then come out and either add up, preserve, or settle-out-of-court with the figures of some well-to-do rough-necks at the wages of a plumber's apprentice when they might go forth and slam some other guy for a goal and drag down about what Woolworth did with a idea and a nickel!

So B.A. from now on will prob'ly stand for "Artistic Bruiser," and when Hiram Briggs, Yale '22, comes home for the holidays the old farm will get a idea of what Belgium had to contend with. Hiram will no doubt greet father with a clout on the chin that will knock the old man kickin', and show the

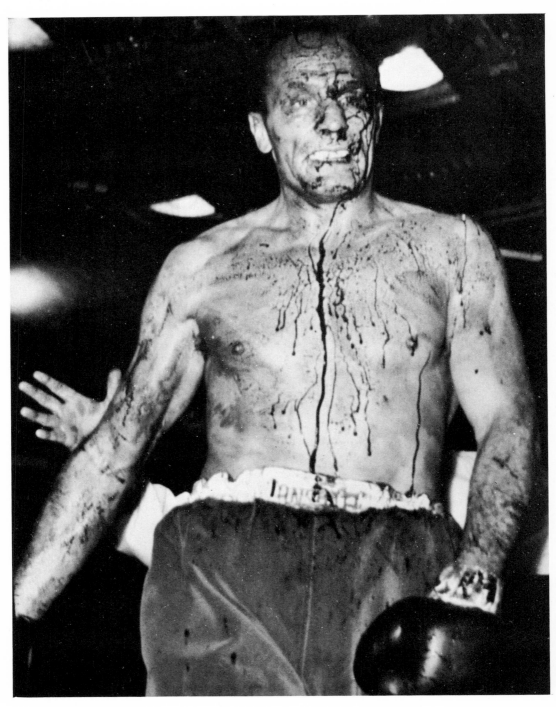

*The "fighting instinct" . . . battering a stranger into a model
for hamburger steak. (Photo of Henry Cooper, after Clay fight.)*

admirin' neighbors the graduation exercises by makin' 'em one and all kiss the turf. He's no doubt liable to bring Professor One-Round Burke, K.O., J.A.B., and H.O.O.K., of the chair of Sockology, home with him, and the Prof. will tell the boy's delighted parents—when they come to—that their son has a bright career ahead of him if he'll only learn to cross with his right after feintin' with his left. I can hear them dotin' parents sayin' now: "My sakes—ain't college wonderful, though? That there professor speaks Greek like a native!" because that's what it'll be to *them*. They may also wonder how the jovial Prof., which has a neck that would make old Bossy's look like a swan's, come by the broken nose and the ear which is a exact reproduction of a cauliflower in mid-season.

But I don't think we will ever have no epidemic of champion prize fighters by the via of dear old Yale drink 'er down, or sweet old fair Harvard, and the etc. The percentage is all against the rah-rah boys, to give 'em a original name, and a ouija into the past will convince the most hysterical that this is as true as a country maiden's heart. This ain't a slam at the college boy— it's a boost. Education is its own punishment. When a guy gets done wadin' through Latin, Greek, Algeometry, Shakespeare, Sanskrit, and How to Leave a Drawin' Room he has also picked up just enough imagination, temperament, and common decency to make it practically impossible for him to go up against some cuckoo which he ain't got a thing against and tear said cuckoo's right ear off for money. In other words, the boy ain't got what the sport writers calls the "fightin' instinct."

From what I been able to discover in several assorted years' connection with the leather-pushin' trade, the "fightin' instinct" consists of batterin' a comparative stranger into a model for hamburger steak, the while splashin' the delighted spectators with the victim's gore, and toppin' the evenin's entertainment off by knockin' him dead the minute he's punch drunk and helpless. Unless you can do that and like it, you'll never get much further along in the ring than wavin' a towel in some other guy's corner. That's the reason that college sensations which has tried their hand at it never set the river on fire as professional sluggers. The guy which has grabbed himself a "Know Ye All by These Presents" from some hotbed of knowledge ain't built to break noses for pieces of eight, and that's that!

These guys which has advanced a coupla years from the days when the monkeys was chucklin' over the human race that was gonna imitate 'em can't work up enough "fightin' instinct" to go in and butcher the party of the second part. If they *do* happen to slap him on the chin, and he starts to shimmy hither and yon about the ring lookin' for a place to lay down and think it over, they step back kinda ashamed they put so much stuff on the wallop and let the poor bimbo recover. The minute either of 'em brings a stream of claret the bout stops and a shakin' of hands is enjoyed by all.

Because the educated guy is lenient with a beaten man he's called "fainthearted," and the sport writers say he'll never get nowheres as a scrapper. Before *he'll* cut a guy's face to crimson ribbons, he's got to be extremely peeved at the victim, otherwise he's just in there for the exercise and sport. The pug is in there for the purpose of aggravated assault—that's his livin', and he goes about it in a businesslike way at all times.

Outside the ring it's all different too. The temperamental baby is liable to fight his head off if you call him a liar—I've known manys the guy which would step outside with Dempsey, and they didn't know as much about box fightin' as I know about the political situation in Hindustan. But how many first-class prize fighters did you ever hear of gettin' mixed up in street *mêlées,* hey? Them guys can't see into this scrappin' for fun no more than Caruso is in the habit of singin' in the subway because he's got a *très bien* voice. Nothin' stirrin'! A prize fighter will fight anybody for money and nobody for anything else. You'd be safer in callin' a roomful of leather pushers a lotta bums than you would given' manys a round-shouldered shippin' clerk a insultin' grin!

SNEAD LOSES 1939 OPEN

by Al Stump and Sam Snead

A leading sports writer of the past decade collaborated (1962) with a golfer of similar stature to recall a figure eight that was not made on a skating rink.

FOR A PLAY-BY-PLAY DESCRIPTION of assorted trap trouble, I can give you the 1939 United States Open Championship held at Spring Mill near Philadelphia. I'll give you this one—and you can keep it. It was the worst experience I've had in my twenty-five tournament years. Spring Mill put the line "to Snead a hole" into the golf book to stay. If I'd murdered someone, I'd have lived it down sooner than the '39 Open.

In the opening two rounds, my 68-71 scores led the field and tied Chick Evans' halfway mark in the Open set at Minikahda back in 1916. A couple of peculiar things happened during these thirty-six holes.

On No. 12 hole, a 480-yard backbreaker, my second shot hooked into a trap guarding the left side of the green. It was a fairly light sand lie, but with a big overhang of shaggy grass above me. The pin was 40 feet away, with little putting surface between the trap exit and cup. I needed quick altitude. Then I needed fast "stop," or backspin. To get both, you take a sand wedge with a wide flange on the bottom and play a cut shot. Here you cut the sand under the ball on the bias, the way a plowshare slices through soil. However, it's not quite the same cut shot you play from deep rough.

Your aim is to come into the ball from the outside in—the same sort of action that produces a slice or fade on a regular shot—and help yourself to a thin cushion of sand under the ball. By bringing the clubhead through on a catercorner angle, you won't bury it in sand and muffle its progress.

In fairway rough, you play the cut shot off the right foot with a very open stance. Your body almost faces the hole, to make certain you get that cutting-across-the-ball action. But in a trap, where you want to take a longer divot to build up that sand cushion, you play the ball more forward, off your left instep.

I guess it almost goes without saying that the clubface never touches the ball in any explosion shot—that you simply are playing a divot of sand out onto the green. Personally, I don't see a golf ball in a trap. I think of it as an extra big grain of sand I want to slip out of there. I aim an inch or two back of the ball and generate plenty of hand speed and fast wrist action at impact with the sand.

73

The biggest "grain" in the trap (the ball) is bound to travel farthest if you don't stop the shot and follow-through until your hands are at least shoulder-high at the finish.

In that No. 12 bunker at Spring Mill, I made sure the face of the wedge was up—or wide open—to get quick loft and altitude. I also slowed down my backswing. Nice lazy timing in a trap pays off, I've found.

And out of the soft sand she popped with the backspin a cut shot gives, and in she rolled for a birdie 3. I've holed longer bunker shots, but none that gave me more of a lift. It made my opening-round 68 possible and did more than that. During the next round, I committed the crime of 4-putting a hole from only 25 feet. Steam started to come out of my ears, but then I thought: *That trap shot yesterday evens up the bad and good breaks—so why worry?*

Going into the final eighteen holes, it looked like I just might win my first National Open. My 212 score tied me with Denny Shute, Clayton Heafner, and Craig Wood, 1 stroke behind Johnny Bulla's first-place 211.

I was loose as a goose, mentally. The night before the final day of play, I did some catsprings and some other calisthenics around the hotel-room floor. My roommate, Gene Sarazen, was already in bed and thought my exercises were tomfoolery.

"This stuff helps me to relax," I told him.

"Yes, and you can sprain your back," said Gene, snapping out the lights and practically ordering me to bed.

I finished my sit-ups in the dark and then slept like a possum in his mother's pouch. I felt another 68 or 69 score coming on when I woke up. Couldn't wait to get out there and win me that $100,000 Open.

With seventy holes played, it looked like I'd make it. Two pars on the finishing holes would give me a 69 for the final round and a seventy-two-hole total of 281. A 281 seemed good enough, as it would tie the all-time Open record. I went for the first par on the seventy-first, where I hit a beautiful 300-yard drive. My second shot was over the green into thick clover grass. Chipping out short, I missed a 5-foot putt by an inch and took a bogey 5.

Right there is where my most famous "blowup" began.

For some reason, nobody wanted to tell me the facts of the situation I was up against—which wasn't anything to worry about. As matters stood, I needed only a par on the last hole to beat the best score registered so far, Byron Nelson's 284, and win. A bogey would tie Nelson. No one else still playing the course was in shape to beat Nelson.

But I didn't know any of this, and my bogey on the seventy-first had made me nervous. Ed Dudley, my playing partner, and others around me knew what Nelson had done, yet not one of them spoke up. When you're in the dark, your fears close in on you. I felt I had to gamble on a birdie on the par-5, 558-yard closing hole.

People were swarming the fairways and I had a thirty-minute, nerve-racking

*"When you need only a bogey 6 to tie for the U.S. Open
. . . and you make an 8, you're ready to take the gas pipe."*

wait while the marshals cleared the way to build up the decision to play that last hole wide open.

The tee shot was hit squarely, but my right hand turned a bit too quickly and the ball started to hook. I said, "Whoa, ball, whoa"—but it hooked into trampled rough anyway. The lie was in sandy soil. Up ahead were traps, short of the green and around it. Normally you'd use an iron to make sure of getting out and up. It was still 275 yards to the pin, however, and I still had the idea that the only way to win was to gamble.

Taking a custom-made 2-wood, with several degrees more loft than a driver, one of my favorite sticks, I went for the pin instead of playing safely out. Hit badly, the ball had no height. It was a low liner pushed down the fairway, and I said, "Giddyap, giddyap," when I saw it failing near a trap 160 yards away.

It fell into the trap. It was partly buried.

Every expert I've read claims that I played the trap shot before I thought it out. That's not true. With 2 shots used up, I had to reach the green with the next (or believed I did) and the green was still 110 yards away. My bunker lie

Illustration by Bruce Stark, New York Daily News

wasn't too bad. Half the ball was visible. Above me the collar of the trap had been resodded with squares of soil topped by rough grass. This lip had to be cleared at a height of about 5 feet. A heavy sand wedge would get me up but wouldn't give me the needed distance. I asked the caddie for a shallower-faced club. "Give me the 8-iron," I said.

Even in 1939, when I was only a two-year touring pro, I knew how risky it can be to use a semilofted iron from a semiburied lie. The danger is that you'll catch the ball too clean. If you don't take enough sand, you don't get it up. Weighing that against the need to reach the green in 3, I gambled.

The ball went 4 feet, slammed into the collar, and stuck in a crack left by the resodding. The moans and groans that went up were nothing to my feeling when I caught it too clean and saw it plug in there. In hitting too clean, you don't get under the ball; you hit too high on it and lose the lofted effect of the club. Now I had to chop sod, grass, ball, and all, while standing on sand below the ball.

To cut it out required a sideswiping blow, and she slashed out to the left 40 yards into another bunker. I was sick all over. Still thinking I needed a birdie on No. 72 to win, all my hopes were gone. In landing in that second trap, I'd used up my birdie shot. And now I was shooting 5 from another tough lie in sand.

Just then somebody stepped out of the gallery and said, "Nelson finished at 284. You've got to get down in two more to tie him."

I thought I'd explode at this news. All those gambling shots had been needless. "Why didn't somebody tell me that back on the tee," I snarled, "so I could play it safe?" I was mad enough to plow through that crowd, swinging a club right and left. People will give you nine million miles of advice when you don't need it, but here in the clutch, they had dummied up on me.

If there's anything in this story I'm not ashamed of, it was the 9-iron recovery I made then. I was shaking all over. But I was still thinking. My ball rested 4 or 5 inches below my feet at the bunker's edge. In any situation where you must stand in the trapside grass with the ball below you, the danger is "falling into" the shot and slicing it. Unless you're careful, because your body is tilted forward, you tend to shift weight too soon from your right leg, on the backswing, to the left leg, on the downswing. Which gives you a push or slice. A photo I have of this Spring Mill explosion shows how I avoided that. I bent my knees more than usual, "sitting down" to the ball. My weight was back on my heels to prevent overshifting. I choked down on the club, to make sure I stayed down to the ball throughout the swing. If you rise up even a little bit on a lie like this, you're ruined. The clubface was closed slightly to counteract any slice. And I scraped the ball onto the green, 40 feet from the cup.

To tie Nelson, I needed the putt, and again I'm not ashamed—the 40-footer came close. It lipped the cup and twisted 3 feet away.

After that, I was an awful sight. I didn't give a damn anymore. The collapse was complete when I missed the 3-footer. One more putt gave me an 8—the most talked-about 8 ever taken in golf, I guess. Some women were crying and men were patting me on the back as I walked to the locker room. It was worse in there. There was dead silence. The other pros avoided looking at me, to spare me embarrassment. The sportswriters stayed far away, too. All except one, George Trevor of New York, who walked up with a pencil and notebook in hand and asked, "Sam, what happened on that last hole?"

The boys led Trevor away before I did something I'd regret. When you need only a bogey 6 to tie for the United States Open Championship, and you make an 8, you're ready to take the gas pipe. My score of 286 was good for third place. Craig Wood and Denny Shute came in later with 284s, to tie Nelson, and Byron then won the play-off.

In my heart I know I'd have won, had somebody briefed me on the true situation back at the seventy-second tee.

That night my old pal, Johnny Bulla, took me under tow and, instead of letting me hide out alone in a hotel room, saw to it that I ate dinner in a public place, then took in a show. "The newspapers will cut you to pieces for this," he warned. "So you'd better start facing it right now."

They stuck it in and broke it off. I was called yellow and a bum and a meathead. The Big Eight never has been forgotten. Fans remember it today when they forget my winning 67-67 finish in the 1949 Masters, or the eagle I shot to beat Jim Ferrier in the 1949 P.G.A. semifinals, or my unbroken string of playoff wins over Ben Hogan, or the 70-70-70 I shot in the closing rounds of the 1947 National Open.

CASEY IN THE BOX

by Meyer Berger

The late prize-winning reporter for The New York Times
poetically described a 1941 World Series crisis.

THE PROSPECTS ALL SEEMED ROSY for the Dodger nine that day.
Four to three the score stood, with one man left to play.
And so, when Sturm died, and Rolfe The Red went out,
In the tall weeds in Canarsie you could hear the Dodgers shout.

A measly few got up to go, a screaming rent the air. The rest
Were held deep-rooted by Fear's gnaw eternal at the human breast.
They thought with only Henrich, Hugh Casey had a cinch.
They could depend on Casey when things stood at the pinch.

There was ease in Casey's manner as he stood there in the box.
There was pride in Casey's bearing, from his cap down to his sox.
And when, responding to the cheers, he took up his trousers' sag,
No stranger in the crowd could doubt, he had them in the bag.

*—the ball rolled far behind, and Henrich speeded
to first base like Clipper on the wind.*

Sixty thousand eyes were on him when Casey toed the dirt.
Thirty thousand tongues applauded as he rubbed his Dodger shirt.
Then while the writhing Henrich stood aswaying at the hip,
Contempt gleamed high in Casey's eye. A sneer curled Casey's lip.

And now the leather-covered sphere came hurtling through the air
And Henrich stood awaiting it, with pale and frightened stare.
Close by the trembling Henrich the ball, unheeded, sped.
"He don't like my style," said Casey. "Strike One!" the umpire said.

From the benches black with people there went up a muffled roar
Like the thunder of dark storm waves on the Coney Island shore.
"Get him!" "Get him, Casey!" shouted someone in the stand.
Hugh Casey smiled with confidence. Hugh Casey raised his hand.

79

With a smile of kindly charity Great Casey's visage shone.
He stilled the Faithful's screaming. He bade the game go on.
He caught Mickey Owen's signal. Once more the spheroid flew.
But Henrich still ignored it. The umpire bawled, "Strike Two!"

"Yay!" screamed the maddened thousands, and the echo answered "YAY!"
But another smile from Casey. He held them under sway.
They saw his strong jaws tighten. They saw his muscles strain,
And they knew that Hughie Casey would get his man again.

Pale as the lily Henrich's lips; his teeth were clenched in hate.
He pounded with cruel violence his bat upon the plate.
And now Great Casey held the ball, and now he let it go.
And Brooklyn's air was shattered by the whiff of Henrich's blow.

But Mickey Owen missed this strike. The ball rolled far behind,
And Henrich speeded to first base, like Clipper on the wind.
Upon the stricken multitude grim melancholy perched.
Dark disbelief bowed Hughie's head. It seemed as if he lurched.

DiMaggio got a single. Keller sent one to the wall.
Two runs came pounding o'er the dish and, oh, this wasn't all.
For Dickey walked and Gordon a resounding double smashed.
And Dodger fans were sickened. All Dodger hopes were dashed.

Oh, somewhere north of Harlem the sun is shining bright.
Bands are playing in The Bronx and up there hearts are light.
In Hunts Point men are laughing, on The Concourse children shout.
But there is no joy in Flatbush. Fate had knocked their Casey out.

Y. A. TITTLE

by Jimmy Breslin

He came lately, and not a day too soon. The sports world badly needed a writer capable of speaking out, loudly and well. This article about Tittle's retirement was written in 1964.

THEY BOTH WOKE UP before the hotel operator rang for them. Y. A. Tittle didn't move. He looked up at the ceiling. This was the last time he would wake up to play a game of football because he has made up his mind to retire. "Costello dogs," he said to himself. He could see the No. 50—a brown 50 on a white jersey. Vince Costello, the Cleveland Browns' linebacker, red-dogs the passer a lot and it was the first thing Y. A. Tittle thought about when he woke up in an eighth-floor room of the Hotel Roosevelt yesterday morning.

It is like that after 27 years. You don't wake up and say "I'm playing today," you wake up and say, "Costello dogs."

"Rain," Thomas said.

"Heavy?" Tittle asked.

"Enough," Thomas said. Thomas opened the window. Tittle could hear the taxicabs down on Madison Avenue, their low pressure tires whining on the wet streets. He reached over to the night table and picked up a thick blue-covered looseleaf notebook. The complete set of Giants' plays are on diagram sheets in the book and Tittle turned to a sheet that said "double dive 35" on the top. It is a straight ahead play and Tittle began to study it. You use straight ahead plays on a muddy field and Y. A. Tittle began to go over every one that the Giants use. The amateur whines and curses the weather that's going to bother his passing. Yesterday morning, Y. A. Tittle looked up football plays that should be used in the mud.

He studied his plays through brown horn-rim glasses that were perched on a big nose that caves in halfway down the left side. Patches of shaved gray hair run down the sides of his bald head. In the back of the neck, the gray runs into deep criss-cross lines. He says he is 38, but the deep wrinkles in the back of the neck tell you that the 38 is just a number that he puts down when they ask him how old he is.

He had spent Friday night the same as he has spent every night before a game since they put television sets into hotel rooms.

Right after dinner, Tittle came back to the hotel room, took off his clothes and sat down to watch television. He was dressed as he always is for television on the night before a game. In his shorts, with the glasses on, a filter-tip cigarette in his hand and his socks on. The socks are always on.

"Lot of years," somebody said to him.

He shook his head. "Twenty-seven," he said. "That's just about my whole life."

"What do you do after tomorrow, give it up?"

"I don't know," he said, "I haven't said anything about it. But this game tomorrow is important to me for a lot of reasons. A lot of reasons. I want to have a good day tomorrow so much . . ."

He wanted to have a good day because it was going to be his last. Y. A. had made up his mind before yesterday's game that he was through. The last thing they like to do is stand and tell strangers who work for newspapers that they are

The end of twenty-seven years.

finished with the business. But they tell each other, and Y. A. Tittle had told them in the dressing room that yesterday was going to be his last game. That would do it, he told them, and on Friday night Tittle sat in his hotel room and he watched television and he kept thinking about the last shot he would ever get. No comebacks, no Cleveland next year. It was Cleveland now, and the career now, so go out right.

Now it was 9:15 in the morning, and Tittle put down the playbook and got up and got dressed for breakfast. He put on a white shirt and solid black tie and dark slacks. He reached into the closet and took out an olive green checked sports jacket.

"Still raining?" he said to Thomas.

Thomas looked out the window. "Raining pretty good," he said.

He took the elevator down to the lobby and walked into the Roosevelt Grill. It is a supper club, but yesterday morning the Giants used it for breakfast. Red-coated waiters served steak and scrambled eggs and the players ate quietly. When they were through, Allie Sherman, the coach, stepped up onto the bandstand. He smoked a cigar and he was in shirt sleeves. A green blackboard had been set up, with red stagelights playing on it.

"Now, once we go to pinch blocking, let each other know when they go back into a zone," Sherman began. He chalked in plays on the board.

In the background, Andy Robustelli's voice could be heard. He was in the back of the room, with the defensive team.

"Remember," his voice said, "we got to kick his rear end in. Remember, kick his rear end in for him."

When Sherman finished, the players filed out. Then Tittle moved over to Sherman's table, put the playbook on it and sat down. Gary Wood, the young one, sat on a chair behind him.

"Well, what do you think?" Tittle asked.

"The Green Bay special should be the best," Sherman said.

"Uh, huh."

Sherman put the cigar in his mouth and waited for another question.

"How do we block on the slant 34?"

"Two-on-one," Sherman said.

Tittle picked up a knife and ran it across the tablecloth. "Now, the biggest frequency of dogging . . ."

"Costello," Sherman said.

"I know," Tittle said.

"This isn't a game you win with the big play," Sherman said. "We have to go straight ahead at them. The longer we have it, the less he does." He was talking about Jimmy Brown; when they are as big as this one they say "he" and never his name.

"Certain types of screens wouldn't be advisable today," Tittle said.

"What ones do you mean?" Sherman asked.

"Well, I don't think to the Frisco side is advisable."

"The Frisco side is all right here."

"I guess I keep thinking of Chicago," Tittle said. He meant last year in the championship game. He tried to throw a sideline screen pass to Phil King, and Ed O'Bradovich, a Chicago lineman, intercepted it and ran for a touchdown.

Sherman smiled. "No, it's different here," he said.

Tittle nodded, "I guess I keep matching a play with a game," he said. "I got a game I can remember for every play that we got. That's the trouble when you've been around a little while. You remember too many games."

It was just like a business conference. There was no talk of "we've got to win" or no worry about getting hurt or how hard he belts when you let him get going for two or three steps. Just two guys sitting at a table and calmly going over technical things.

Football, when you do it for money, is like this. It is a trade, a job for money, and in all of New York few people ever have done their jobs better than Y. A. Tittle. They brought him into this town to pass a football and he did it well enough to bring the Giants to three championship games. But this year, with age taking a step away from him, and leaving him standing there a target for a lineman, he has done little.

John Baker of Pittsburgh got to him in the second game and tore two of his ribs loose, and after that the Giants were through and Y. A. Tittle had to gasp for breath every time he tried a pass. Yesterday, he was ready. The pain was gone, and there was a shot of cortisone in him to keep it out. The Browns were coming in for a game which meant the league title for them. Tittle was coming in after something, too.

He had done too much around here to walk out of this town a loser. He plays football in the big place, New York, the only town in the world worth talking about, and yesterday he wanted to go out of the town on top.

"You only know what it's like to play around here if you've played someplace else first," he was saying at the table. "This is the city for an athlete. I don't think I can remember a game I think is as important as this one to me."

The bus left for the ball park at 11:15. Tittle sat in the back, on the right, a thumbnail between his teeth, looking out the window. He ran a hand over the glass so he could see out. He looked down at the sidewalk. Rain splashed into a puddle alongside the doorman.

Tittle began to move his lips.

The opener, he was saying to himself. Open with a double dive 39. Wheelwright right at them. Straight ahead. And watch Costello. Watch what he does on the play. You want to know what he's doing.

In the stadium, in the light-green-carpeted dressing room, he put on a gray sweatshirt and sat on a stool and looked down at his legs. Tittle's legs were smooth shaven, so tape can be put all over them and then ripped off once a day. His toes stick together, with corns on the sides, the toenails black from 260-pound linemen stepping on them all year.

"I saw you in the first game you ever played here," somebody said to him. "It was on a Thursday night, against the Yankees." Tittle smiled. The guy was talking about the old football Yankees.

"What about the kids?" he was asked. "Do they think it's funny that this might be your last game?"

"I don't know," he said. "They're used to this business. Kids can adjust when they're used to things. My daughter now, she takes American history here. Then next week we get back to Palo Alto, she'll be having world history. Everything changes and she just keeps up with it."

Then he got up and started to get dressed, and the thumbnail came up to his teeth again and he began to think about another play.

At 12:45, a buzzer rang in the room. It meant the players had to get up and get ready to go on the field and everybody came around and tapped Y. A. on the shoulder and wished him luck and he sat there quietly and said thank you, and pulled on a cigarette he had cupped in his hand so photographers wouldn't catch him smoking. It was, it seemed, just another working day for him.

Then you shook hands with him and your hand closed on wetness. His whole palm was wet.

"What's this?" he was asked.

"This?" he smiled. "This is the business."

And a few minutes later, clapping his hands together, Tittle came trotting out of the dressing room, down the runway to the baseball dugout and then up the stairs and onto the field, and there was a huge roar from the crowd when he came running through the goalposts and over to the bench. He waited while the Giants took the kick-off and when that was over Y. A. came running on the field for the last big shot of his career. He wanted to go out of this city the way the good ones always do. The field was all right, and the rain was almost gone. He had a shot at it. A good shot at going out of this town on top. He bent his head into the huddle and called the first play of the game—a double dive 39.

Tittle took the snap, spun, handed the ball to Ernie Wheelwright and then kept going back, faking a pass. He kept looking over his shoulder at the Browns as he did. What he saw was no good. Their line jumped the Giants on this first play and Wheelwright ran into three or four white jerseys and right away, yesterday afternoon, you could see Y. A. Tittle was going to have trouble.

For the Browns kept getting that first step on the Giants' line and they stacked up runs and their halfbacks were all over the Giants' receivers. And on offense, they simply shoved everybody out and let him smash. He smashed and spun off them, Jimmy Brown did, and they were defenseless against him, and the Browns had the ball too much of the time.

In the second quarter, with the Browns ahead, 3–0, Tittle went back and saw nobody open and then he said the hell with it. He took off on his own to the right and got to the Browns' 18. Ross Fichtner got to him near the sideline and tried to break him in half. Y. A. went down face first into the mud, but he pulled himself up right away. The referee was yelling about a personal foul and the ball was going to be put on the Cleveland 9. Now Tittle didn't hurt at all from the tackle.

On the second play, somebody was after him from the side, and Tittle ran straight up. Then he stopped and threw to Dick James, who was a yard behind the goal line. That put the Giants ahead, 7–3, and Tittle had spring in his legs when he ran back to the bench.

The Browns came back and scored. Ryan, their quarterback, was having a big day. Then Tittle was on the field again and he hit Joe Morrison on the Browns' 49 and now noise came down out of the three-decked green stands. Tittle clapped his hands and bent down in the huddle. He wanted Gifford this time, he told them. They broke out of the huddle and Tittle loped up to the line, looking over the Browns as he came. Steam was coming off his face and out of his mouth into the dark, wet air. He stood behind the center, Mickey Walker, and looked around. The old pro was working his trade now.

Mickey Walker's gray pants were straining as he bent over the ball. The others were there, too. Bookie Bolin, Darrell Dess. At the snap, they would be coming back to make a pocket for Y. A. Tittle. Gifford was out on the right. Tittle put his hands down. The Cleveland halfbacks, Walter Beach, over on the left, and Bernie Parrish, on the right, were deep. They go even deeper when you show pass. Good. Tittle had called Gifford on a square-cut to the sidelines in front of Parrish.

Y. A. got the ball on the two-count and went straight back. Walker, Dess and Bolin came back with him and the white jerseys rushed at the three and grunted and slammed and tried to get through. Tittle turned around and held the ball up. Here was Gifford faking deep, throwing his head to the left, then cutting in one motion and running for the sideline, and Y. A. Tittle threw it at him and everything he wanted out of yesterday afternoon was in that pass.

Gifford was at the Browns' 34 and he had his hands out and the ball was coming right to him when Parrish came running right by him and grabbed the ball and took off down the sidelines with the Browns' bench screaming "Ball!" to let their players on the field know there was an interception and to start blocking.

Tittle already was on his way over to the sidelines. You learn how to do this back in high school, in Marshall, Texas. You always get over there and cover the sidelines when you throw a pass out there. Y. A. Tittle put his head down and ran straight for the sidelines, at the Giants' 30, and Parrish was trying to get past that spot and into the open. Tittle came up and he threw his body at Parrish's legs, and Parrish went up in the air and came down on his shoulder. The two of them

. . . he took off on his own, and they tried
to break him in half.

skidded in the deep mud and then Parrish jumped up and clapped his hands and the Browns' offensive team was coming on the field and it was all over.

Sometimes, it goes like that. Everything can be all right and you can know just what has to be done and how to do it, and you've done it a lot of times before and it has worked, and then when you do it this time the whole thing falls apart. It is like that in any business office in the city. Even the best in the place falls apart on something. Y. A. Tittle, who worked at his trade in New York as well as any ever worked, had just blown it all on a play called a square-cut. He has been pulling these off for 27 years.

At the end, Tittle was on one knee in front of the Giants' bench, a blue hood thrown over his shoulders, his hands scraped and mud caked. The lights were reflecting off the puddles in the mud around him. Out on the field, Gary Wood was running the team, and the Browns, scoring nearly every time they got the ball, ran up a 52–20 victory.

"How is it?" he was asked.

He shook his head.

"I'm sorry," somebody said to him.

"I'm sorry I couldn't give you something better," he said. "You people here have been awful nice to me."

He walked out of the stadium an hour later, in a black raincoat and black tyrolean hat with a red feather in it. He carried a brown leather attache case and he looked like a businessman coming home from work, which is what he is going to be from now on. Yesterday was the last shot of a career that went 27 years and he blew it on a play called a square-cut. Y. A. Tittle said he was sorry he couldn't have given the people a little more. Professionals think that way.

THE DEATH OF MANOLETE

by Barnaby Conrad

Author-Illustrator, aficionado of "la fiesta brava,"
Conrad wrote this story of a matador's death in 1950.

MANUEL LAUREANO RODRIGUEZ Y SANCHEZ, called Manolo by his friends, "The Monster" by the press, and known to the adoring public of three continents as Manolete, the world's greatest bullfighter, was drunk. A stranger might not have noticed it, but I knew he didn't talk this much or this confidentially. Especially when sober.

"I'm quitting," he said in his low Cordoban accent. He said it vehemently, as though expecting someone to come back with "Oh, yeah?"

He stood up, glancing over at his mistress, and went to the window of my apartment. He stared out at the Peruvian sunset and nervously shook the ice in his empty glass as though it were dice.

"I tell you, *compadre,* I'm through with it all. I'm going back to Spain and cut off the pigtail forever. I've made more money than five generations of my family put together, but I've never had time to spend it. I'm young. Twenty-nine's not old. I've had my horn wounds, but I'm still in one piece, *gracias a Dios.*"

A short scar notched the left side of his chin, and he put his fingers to it unconsciously. His face, ugly when analyzed feature by feature, was sad and drawn and old, yet at the same time it was compeling and majestic. If he were to walk into any café in any part of the world, people would immediately ask: Who is this gaunt young-old man—for he had the look and aura of Number One. Hod-carrier, dancer, artist, banker, one might not know—only that he was the best in his field.

He ran long fingers over the black hair that had a wide path of gray down the center. "I've been able to spend about three months on my place in Cordoba in all the years I've owned it. I'm going back and enjoy it—never look at another bull except from up in the stands."

He went out to the pantry for another drink, and I turned to Antonia Bronchalo, for several years his "fiancée." She was pretty and seemed like a

89

nice girl, but people said she was hard as Toledo steel. She'd made a few Spanish movies under the name of Lupe Sino, but she was no star. Her fame would always rest in the fact that she was loved by important men—lots of them.

"What do you think," I asked. "Will he quit?"

She smiled. "He's told me for several months now that he'll give it up the moment we get back to Spain and that we'll get married and raise bulls and half a dozen little Manoletes. He's starting to slip. He should get out quick, alive. But they'll never let him." She looked up at the portrait I had done of him. "That pretty gold uniform means excitement and money to too many people for them ever to let him take it off. They'll kill him first."

She was right. When Manolete arrived back in Spain in the spring of 1947, he received a tremendous reception. As the papers put it, no one since the conquistadors had so successfully carried the glories of Spain to the New World. Then, after he announced he was going to retire, they set about to kill him.

It's hard for Americans to understand why all this fuss about one bull-fighter. But he wasn't just a bullfighter to the Spaniards. He was their only national and international hero. We have Eisenhower, Gable, Grable, DiMaggio and hundreds of others, but they just had Manolete. And when he was killed, he died such a beautiful dramatic Spanish death that I swear, in spite of the great funeral, the week of national mourning, the odes, the dirges, the posthumous decorations by the government, that in his heart of hearts every Spaniard was glad that he had died.

He even looked Quixotic. Ugly in photos, cold and hard in the bull ring, he had tremendous magnetism, warmth, and gentle humor among his friends. Once in Peru I took a blasé American college girl to watch Manolete in the ceremony of preparing for a fight, though she protested she had no interest in a "joker who hurts little bulls."

"Excuse me, Señorita, if I don't talk much," he said with his shy smile as they worried his thin frame into the skin-tight uniform, "but I am very scared."

After that he didn't say more than ten words to her. But she walked out of the room dazed. "That," she announced, "is the most attractive man in the world."

"To fight a bull when you are not scared is nothing," another bullfighter once said, "and to not fight a bull when you are scared is nothing. But to fight a bull when you are scared—that is something."

Manolete told me: "My knees start to quake when I first see my name on the posters and they don't stop until the end of the season."

But there was never any real end of the season for him. In 1945, for example, he fought ninety-three fights in Spain in six months, about one every other day. This meant body-racking travel, for he would fight in Barcelona one day, Madrid the next, and then maybe Lisbon the day after. He would snatch some sleep in the train or car and sometimes had to board a plane with his ring outfit still on. Then followed Mexico's season and Peru's season and when he got through with those it was March again and time for the first fights in Valencia.

What, then, made him run? What made him The Best?

Money was the obvious thing. In his eight years as a senior matador he made approximately four million American dollars. In his last years he was getting as high as $25,000 per fight, about $400 for every minute he performed, and he could fight where, when, and as often as he liked. His yearly income was slightly abetted by such things as a liqueur called Anis Manolete, dolls dressed in costume with his sad face on them, testimonials for cognac ads, songs about him, and a movie called *The Man Closest to Death*.

Yet it wasn't the money; people seldom risk their necks just for money. It was that he needed desperately to be someone—something great.

He was born in Cordoba, Spain, in 1917, in the heart of the bullfighting country. His great uncle, a minor-league bullfighter, was killed by a bull, one of the dreaded Miura breed that years later was to kill Manuel. His mother was the widow of a great matador when she married Manuel's father, also a bullfighter. He began to go blind, kept fighting as long as he could distinguish the shape of the bull, and finally died in the poorhouse when Manuel was five years old.

The family was always hungry-poor. Manuel was a frail child, having had pneumonia when a baby, and could contribute little to his mother's support. But he started carrying a hod as soon as he was big enough to tote one.

His two sisters stood the hunger as long as possible and then they started making money in a profession even older than bullfighting. This was the secret of the driving force behind Manuel. He never got over it. He resolved to make enough money somehow so that his family would never have to worry again, and to become an important enough person so that his sisters' shame would be blurred. Bullfighting is the only way in Spain for a poor boy to become great. "Matadors and royalty are the only ones who live well," they say. Young Manuel decided to become the greatest bullfighter who ever lived.

He was 12 and working as a plasterer's assistant on the Sotomayor ranch when he got his first chance. They raised fighting bulls, that special savage breed of beast, originally found only on the Iberian peninsula, that can kill a lion or tiger easily and which the Caesars used to import for the Coliseum orgies. Little Manuel begged so persistently to be allowed to fight that finally the Sotomayors put him in the corral with a cape and a yearling. Manuel, an awkward, skinny kid in short pants, was knocked down every time he went near the little animal. If the animal had had sharp horns instead of stubs, he would have been killed twenty times; instead he was just a mass of bruises by the time he limped out of the ring. He decided to go back to plastering.

But he couldn't stay away from the bulls. In the next few years he got out with the calves every time he could, even after he had been badly wounded, at 13, by a young bull. There are always backseat bullfighters around a ranch and they told him some of the mistakes he was making. He learned fairly fast but he was no genius. He was awkward and tried to do the wrong kind of passes for his build. However, he was brave and took it so seriously that he finally persuaded someone to give him a fight with small bulls in Cordoba's big Plaza de Toros under the *nom de toreau* of Manolete.

In his debut he was clumsy, but so brave and obviously trying so hard that the home folks applauded the sad-faced gawk. It was the greatest day of his life. Flushed with success, he and two other boys scraped their money together, formed a team called the Cordoban Caliphs, and set out to make their fortune. They wangled some contracts fighting at night and in cheap fairs and traveled around Spain for a year. Manolete was almost the comic relief of the outfit. The crowds would laugh at his skinny frame, made more awkward by the fancy passes he was trying. His serious, ugly face and his earnestness made it all the funnier.

"He looks as dreary as a third-class funeral on a rainy day," they'd say. But they couldn't laugh at the way he killed. He was so anxious to do well that when it came time to dispatch his enemy, Manolete would hurl himself straight over the lowered head, the horn missing his body by inches, to sink the sword up to the hilt between the shoulders.

"He's going to get killed that way some day," said the experts, prophetically.

His career, if you could call it that at this point, was interrupted by his being drafted into the army. After his discharge a year later he resumed fighting without the other two Caliphs. Then came the turning point in his life, for Camara spotted him.

José Flores Camara, a bald, dapper little man of 35 with omnipresent dark glasses, might have become the greatest bullfighter of all time except for one thing: He was a coward. He displayed more grace and knowledge of bull psychology than anyone had ever seen before. He had the build and he knew all about the different fighting habits of bulls and the rest of the complicated science of tauromachy. The only thing he couldn't do was keep his feet from dancing back out of the way when the bull charged, which is the most important thing in bullfighting.

When he happened to see Manolete gawking around a small-town ring, he knew that here was someone who could be everything that he had failed to be. With his expert eye he saw what the crowd didn't, that the boy wasn't really awkward, but that he was trying the wrong passes for his build and personality. Camara figured that with his brains and Manolete's blood they

". . . but to fight a bull when you are scared—that is something."

could really go places. He signed up the astonished young man for a long, long contract.

Camara remade Manolete. He took him out to the ranches and showed him what he was doing wrong. He made him concentrate on just the austere classic passes, none of the spinning or cape-twirling ones. With the cape he showed him how to do beautiful show veronicas, finishing with a half-veronica. It was the only pass, of the dozens that exist, that Manolete would ever do again with the cape. With the small muleta cape used with the sword, Camara let him do only four passes. He showed him how to hold himself regally, how to give the classic passes with a dignity never before seen in the ring.

When Camara thought he was ready, he launched his protégé. It took a little while for people to appreciate what they were witnessing, but soon they came to realize that here was a revolutionary, a great artist. His repertory was startlingly limited, but when he did the simple veronica the cape became a live thing in his hands, and the easy flow of the cloth, the casual way it brought the bull's horns within a fraction of an inch of his legs, was incredibly moving. Heightening the effect was the serious mien and the cold face, not unlike Basil Rathbone's, that gave a feeling of tragedy every time he went into the ring. No one laughed at him now. Camara had made a genius out of a clown. And always the nervous little man with his dark glasses was behind the fence while his protégé was out with the bull watching every move and saying: "Careful, Manolo, this one will hook to the left," or "Take him on the other side, he has a bad eye" or "Fight him in the center, he swerves when he's near the fence." And Manolete kept learning and learning.

If his first year was successful, his second was sensational. It seemed as though Spain had just been waiting for his kind of fighting. His honest and brave style seemed to show up the fakery that the cape-twirlers had been foisting upon the public. In 1939 he took "the alternative" and became a senior matador, fighting older and larger bulls. From then on his rise was dizzy, for every fight and every season seemed better than the last one.

By 1946 he was the king of matadors and Mexico beckoned with astronomical contracts, the highest prices ever paid a bullfighter. Spectators thought they were lucky to get a seat for $100 for his first fight in Mexico City. It was the greatest responsibility a matador ever had, and he gave them their money's worth, although he was carried out badly wounded before the fight was half over. He came to before they got him to the ring infirmary, shook off the people who tried to stop him, and lurched back into the ring to finish the bull, before collapsing.

After he recovered he went on to fight all over Mexico and South America. When I saw him in Lima he was exhausted. Most bullfighters can give a top performance one day and then get away with a few safe, easy ones. But not Manolete. To preserve his fabulous reputation he had to fight every fight as though it were his first time in the Madrid Plaza.

But the machine was wearing down. Though he was only 29, he looked 40. He was drinking a lot, and not mild Spanish wine but good old American whisky. His timing was beginning to go off. I remember once in Peru he took nine sword thrusts to kill a bull, and he left the ring with tears running down his cheeks.

Even Camara, who enjoyed having his wallet filled through risks taken by someone else, thought it was time to quit. But the public makes an idol and then it tires of what it has made and destroys the idol. When Manolete returned to Spain and announced that he was going to retire, he found he had slipped from public grace. The people were saying that he had dared only to fight small bulls and that this new young Luis Miguel Dominguin was better and braver. Manolete had been on top too long. They wanted someone new. They amused themselves by changing the words of the once-popular eulogizing song "Manolete" to: "Manolete, you couldn't handle a robust field mouse if confronted by one in the bathroom."

"Quit," Camara advised him. "Quit," said Luis Miguel, who would then be cock of the roost. "Quit," said the other bullfighters who then wouldn't look so clumsy and cowardly.

Manolete had too much pride to quit under fire. He said he would have one last season, just a few short months, with the largest bulls in Spain, and fighting with any fighters the promoters wished to bill him with. He wanted to retire untied and undefeated.

His first fight was in Barcelona, and the critics said he had never been greater. Then Pamplona, and he was even better than at Barcelona. It looked as though everyone was wrong, that he was in his prime.

Then, on July 16, he was wounded, in Madrid. The wound wasn't serious, but he left the hospital too soon to go on a vacation in the mountains with Antonia. He began fighting again long before he should have; it was as though he were afraid that if he missed any of these last contracts there would always be some people who would remain unconvinced that he was still The Best.

The next fights were not good. He just wasn't up to it physically, and he wasn't helping himself by the way he was drinking. He would stay up all night with a bottle of whisky, not go to bed, and try to fight the next afternoon. They say he drank because of Antonia, because he knew she was a girl "of a bad style" and a gold digger, but that he loved her and couldn't break off with her and hated himself for loving her. A friend of his said, "She dragged poor Manolo through the Street of Bitterness with her cheapness."

Also the crowds' new attitude toward him was intolerable, not because of egotism but because of his professional pride. Now they were always prone to applaud the other matadors more, no matter how close Manolete let death come.

"They keep demanding more and more of me in every fight," he complained. "And I have no more to give."

The Manolete myth had grown bigger than the real Manolete, and the people were angry at him instead of at themselves for having created it.

Then came August 27, and the fight in Linares. It was extremely important to him that he be good this afternoon. First, because it was near his home town; second, because Luis Miguel Dominguin was on the same program; third, because the bulls were Miuras, the famous "bulls of death" that have killed more men than any other breed in existence. People claimed that Manolete was scared of Miuras and had always avoided fighting them.

Since it was midsummer and the sun shines till 9 in Andalusia, the fight didn't begin until 6:30. It began like any other of his fights—the stands jammed with mantilla-draped señoritas and men with the broad-brimmed somberos cocked over one eye. There was an excitement in the air because of the Miuras and the known rivalry between Dominguin and Manolete.

Gitanillo did well by the first bull and received applause and handkerchief waving, which meant the audience wanted him to be granted an ear of the dead bull as a token of a good performance. But the president was hard to please and refused to grant it.

The second bull was Manolete's. It was dangerous and unpredictable, but Manolete was out to cut an ear. He made the animal charge back and forth in front of him so closely and gracefully that even his detractors were up out of their seats, yelling. But when it came time to kill, he missed with the first thrust. The second dropped the bull cleanly and the crowd applauded wildly, but he had lost the ear.

The trumpet blew, and it was Luis Miguel's turn. This was an important fight to him also. He wanted to show up the old master in his own province. He wanted to show them who could handle Miuras better than anyone in the world.

He strode out into the arena, good-looking, smug, 20 years old. Manolete was through—here was the new idol, here was the king of the rings!

He had the crowd roaring on the first fancy, twirling passes with the big cape. He put in his own *banderillas* superbly to win more applause. With the muleta, the little cape that is draped over the sword for the last part of the fight, he unfurled all of his crowd-pleasing tricks, dropping to his knees for two passes and even kissing the bull's forehead at one moment. He lined the bull up, thrust the sword in between the withers halfway up to the hilt, and the animal sagged down dead. The crowd cheered and waved their handkerchiefs until the president granted Dominguin an ear.

Manolete had watched the entire performance from the passageway, with no change of expression. Those tricks and cape twirls were not his idea of true bullfighting. He would show the crowd what the real thing was if it killed him.

After Gitanillo's mediocre performance with his second animal, Manolete saw the toril gate swing open and the last bull of his life came skidding out of the tunnel. It was named Islero, and it was big and black with horns as sharp as needles. The moment Camara saw it hooking around the ring, he sucked in his breath and said to Manolete: "*Malo*—bad, bad. It hooks terribly to the right." That is a dread thing, for a matador must go over to the right horn to kill. "Stay away from this one, *chico*."

But Manolete was determined to give the best performance of his life. He caught the collar of the cape in his teeth and held it while he got the big scarlet cloth right in his hands. Then he slid through the opening in the fence and called the bull.

"Toro, hah, torooo!" he called in his deep voice, holding the cape out in front of him and shaking it.

The animal wheeled at the voice, its tail shot up, and it charged across the ring. As it reached the cloth the man didn't spin or swirl the cape around him or dance around the way that Luis Miguel had done. He merely planted his feet and swung the cape slowly in front of the bull's nose, guiding the great head with the tantalizing cloth so that the left horn went by his legs ten inches away. Without moving his feet, he took the bull back in another charge and the right horn stabbed six inches away from his thighs. Five more perfect classic veronicas, each closer than the other, finishing with a half-veronica that was so close that the bull's neck hit him and nearly knocked him off balance. He turned his back on the bewildered animal and looked up at the crowd that was cheering deliriously, a crowd that had been shown the difference between truth and fakery.

With the muleta cape, his forte, he worked in even closer, until the crowd was shouting, "No, no!" Camara was shouting with them, for Manolete was passing the animal just as closely on the right side as the left. But the man didn't pay any attention. He did the Pass of Death and his own pass, the dangerous "manoletina." He did fifteen suicidal "natural" passes, the one where the sword is taken out of the cape and only the limp bit of rag is used to divert the bull's charge away from the body. Then he did his famous trade-mark— the fantastic pass where he looked disdainfully away from the bull up into the stands as the animal thundered by. It seemed as though the bull couldn't miss, but it did. By now the crowd was hoarse from cheering the domination that the man had acquired over the wild beast.

It was time to kill. As he was lining up the Miura so that the feet would be together and the shoulder blades open, Camara and his *banderilleros* were yelling: "Stay away from him, man! Off to the side and get away quick!"

But Manolete had to finish this one right. He wasn't going to spoil the performance by running off to the side and stabbing it in the lungs. He was going to head in straight, get the sword in, give the bull a fair shot at him, and hope to God it wouldn't hook to the right.

He stood in front of the Miura, sighted down the blade, rose on the toes of one foot, and as the bull lunged forward, Manolete hurled himself straight over the lowered right horn. The sword was sinking in, the horn cutting by him. But suddenly the bull wrenched its head to the right and drove the horn deep into the man's groin. Manolete was flung high into the air, trying to fight the horn out of his body, and then was slammed to the sand. The bull spiked at him twice on the ground and then staggered, choked, and flopped over dead, the sword up to the red hilt between its shoulder blades.

The pool of blood on the sand told them the man was mortally wounded. Camara and the *banderilleros* picked up the unconscious form and rushed him down the passageway to the ring infirmary. He came to on the operating table and gasped weakly: "Did it die?"

"*Si, chico, si,*" said Camara, tears raining down his cheeks.

"It died and they didn't give me anything?" Manolete said, trying to raise himself from the table.

"They gave you everything, Matador," said a *banderillero,* putting his cigarette between the wounded man's lips. "Everything—both ears and tail."

He smiled and lay back.

Antonia arrived from Granada at 3:30 in the morning and demanded a deathbed wedding ceremony, but his friends wouldn't allow it; Manolete's money would go to his family.

At 5 in the morning he moaned: "Doctor, I can't feel anything in my right leg." The doctor assured him he would be well in no time. Then: "Doctor, I can't feel anything in my left leg." He gave a cry and said: "I can't see!" and he was dead.

An old *banderillero* staring at the corpse said dully: "They kept demanding more and more of him, and more was his life, so he gave it to them."

WHEN THE NEWS ARRIVED

by James Murray

A Los Angeles Times *writer catches the inner drama of Hogan's thwarted bid for an unprecedented fifth U.S. Open crown in a 1955 playoff.*

In the locker room, Ben Hogan sank heavily on a bench and took a Scotch and water from somebody's hand. It seemed certain that his 287 had clinched his fifth championship. He sipped his drink, shook his head and said slowly: "Boys, if I win it, I'll never work at this again. It's just too tough getting ready for a tournament. This one doggone near killed me. Besides, I don't think it's fair to drag Valerie [Mrs. Hogan] around and put her through this every time." Someone asked if his leg had bothered him. "Only my knee," said Ben. "The more I walked, the more it hurt." From the end of the row of lockers an attendant shouted: "Jack Fleck is on 16 and he needs one birdie on the last three to tie!" Hogan sipped his drink, then smiled thinly: "Good for him." A reporter asked: "Which hole do you think you won it on, Ben?" He frowned: "There's no one hole. You don't win tournaments on just one hole. There's 72 holes." A newcomer burst into the group. "Fleck's parred 17!" he cried. "Just missed his birdie. Needs a birdie on 18 to tie." Hogan stood up. He stepped out of his slacks, revealing a bandaged left knee. "I got to take a shower," he said. He walked off, stiff-legged. There was small talk, then the group was silent until Ben returned. He pulled on his slacks, slipped on his tasseled shoes, grinned as he looked around. Another runner arrived, panting. "Fleck's in the rough on the 18th," he shouted. Everyone turned back to Hogan. He reached into his locker, pulled out his tie and slowly began knotting it. Incredibly, somebody decided to ask: "Ben, did you use your own clubs, the ones you manufacture, in the tournament?" Hogan whirled and exploded: "Of course I did! Are you kidding?" Jack Burke walked in, began to wrestle with his locker. "What did you do, boy?" Hogan called to him. "No good, Ben," Burke answered. "Drove in the rough all day." Tommy Bolt came in, elaborately avoided Topic A: "Hey, Benny, you got me all fouled up down there at Fort Worth. You got me to fix that hook. Now, doggone it, I'm slicing the ball. I'm goin' back to hookin'. You son of a gun, I bet you did that a-purpose." Hogan smiled. Cary Middlecoff appeared, stuck out his hand.

99

"Wonderful tournament, Ben, wonderful," he said. "A damn good score." He hurried away. Hogan drew on his jacket, reached into his locker and took out his clubs and threw them on the floor. "Anybody want a club cover?" he asked affably. Before anyone could answer, a new informant rushed in. "Ben, Fleck's got an eight-foot putt to tie!" Hogan relaxed. No one could think of anything to say for a moment. Then, desperately, a man brought up the subject of Ben's club manufacturing business again. "Now, how many clubs will you make in a day, Ben?" he asked. "It comes to 460 sets a month, Bill," Hogan said. "Isn't it true, Ben," the man rushed on, "that you threw away a hundred thousand clubs because they weren't perfect?" Hogan nodded. "I got at least $150,000 worth of

". . . If I win it, I'll never work at this again."

The kid sank it!

new clubs I won't ship." He sat down on the bench again. The group fell silent.
Then it came: a tremendous roar of the gallery at the 18th. A reporter whispered
hoarsely: "The kid's sunk it!" Ben Hogan's head went down and he cursed softly.
Then he lifted his head and looked around at them all. "I was wishing he'd either
make a two or a five," he said. "I was wishing it was over—all over." He turned
to an attendant, indicated his clubs and sighed. "Well, we might as well git those
things back in the locker. Gotta play tomorrow, looks like."

PARET UNDER KNIFE

by Leonard Lewin

The grim death of a fighter in 1962, by one of the nation's top boxing analysts.

A MOMENT OF EXCITEMENT as Emile Griffith hammered at Benny "The Kid" Paret unmercifully in a corner . . . then a tragic silence . . .

The shocking end came so swiftly that Griffith didn't immediately grasp the seriousness of the situation and struggled with his handlers to get at Paret for more.

When referee Ruby Goldstein rushed in to pull an excited Griffith away, Paret's unconscious body slipped to the floor, rolled over and began quivering. Goldstein managed to tug the squirming Griffith halfway to his corner, and then rushed back to help the Kid.

Meanwhile, Griffith was trying to break free from his handlers and get at Paret. Why? he was asked later.

"He called me a nasty name in my last two fights and at the weigh-in," the 25-year-old Griffith said after regaining the crown he'd lost to Paret in last December's hotly disputed decision. "I wanted to get back at him before the referee stopped the fight. I didn't want to hurt him that way. I just wanted him down so that the referee couldn't stop it. I didn't know he was down."

Seconds later, Griffith stood in the middle of the ring crying as the photographers popped the traditional victory picture. It was a macabre contrast: Emile, standing with his arm raised and a hand wiping away tears, while a group of doctors worked feverishly over the prostrate Paret.

Why didn't Goldstein stop it sooner? Should he have stepped in before he did—while the crazed Griffith was uppercutting and then smashing Paret, helpless against the ropes?

"I didn't think the uppercuts were doing any damage," said the highly respected veteran referee who, ironically, has a reputation for stopping fights too soon.

"I was expecting him to weave out of the corner, as he had done all through the fight. But when I saw Griffith hit him while his head was between the ropes, and he didn't respond, I rushed in as fast as I could.

102

In blind rage . . . in victory . . . in tears.

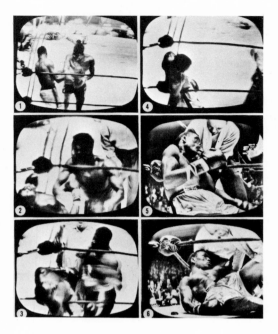

"These things pile up. No one punch does the damage. This was a championship fight and I realize that people want to give the champion every opportunity. That's what I was trying to do . . ."

Actually, there were very few people on hand that night who could honestly say they would have stopped it sooner. Paret had consistently fought out of danger in the grudge battle that brought repeated foul warnings, especially to the Kid.

In the sixth, for example, after Griffith had punished him for five straight rounds, the Kid dumped Emile for a count of eight. It happened fifteen seconds before the bell, and Griffith was able to stagger through the round.

That one blow took so much steam out of the aggressive and sharp Griffith that he was only a shell until the tragic twelfth. It was anyone's fight till then. Paret had him backing away when it happened.

The Kid got tagged in the middle of the ring and gave ground.

Griffith went after him with all the pent-up fury and hate for the man who had insulted him. He stormed Paret into the corner with a series of head blows. Then, as the Kid stood there, Griffith rocked his head back and forth with uppercut after uppercut. They weren't powerful, but they were undefended. Paret's arms hung over the ropes. Griffith now was in a blind rage. He stepped back and bounced his gloved fists off the Kid's head as though it were the light punching bag.

Goldstein was standing close by . . . he rushed in and grabbed Griffith. But the damage was done. Who can really say when it was done?

What difference does it make now? It's not going to help Paret win the most important fight of his career . . . the fight for his life.

THE
WINNERS

UNDERTAKER SONG

by Damon Runyon

About the Harvard-Yale game in 1934 and some of the
"Guys and Dolls" who attended same for a variety of reasons.

Now this story I am going to tell you is about the game of football, a very healthy pastime for the young, and a great character builder from all I hear, but to get around to this game of football I am compelled to bring in some most obnoxious characters, beginning with a guy by the name of Joey Perhaps, and all I can conscientiously say about Joey is you can have him.

It is a matter of maybe four years since I see this Joey Perhaps until I notice him on a train going to Boston, Mass., one Friday afternoon. He is sitting across from me in the dining-car, where I am enjoying a small portion of baked beans and brown bread, and he looks over to me once, but he does not rap to me.

There is no doubt but what Joey Perhaps is bad company, because the last I hear of him he is hollering copper on a guy by the name of Jack Ortega, and as a consequence of Joey Perhaps hollering copper, this Jack Ortega is taken to the city of Ossining, N.Y., and placed in an electric chair, and given a very, very, very severe shock in the seat of his pants.

It is something about plugging a most legitimate business guy in the city of Rochester, N.Y., when Joey Perhaps and Jack Ortega are engaged together in a little enterprise to shake the guy down, but the details of this transaction are dull, and sordid, and quite uninteresting, except that Joey Perhaps turns state's evidence and announces that Jack Ortega fires the shot which cools the legitimate guy off, for which service he is rewarded with only a small stretch.

I must say for Joey Perhaps that he looks good, and he is very well dressed, but then Joey is always particular about clothes, and he is quite a handy guy with the dolls in his day and, to tell the truth, many citizens along Broadway are by no means displeased when Joey is placed in the state institution, because they are generally pretty uneasy about their dolls when he is around.

Naturally, I am wondering why Joey Perhaps is on this train going to Boston, Mass., but for all I know maybe he is wondering the same thing about me, although personally I am making no secret about it. The idea is I am en route to Boston, Mass., to see a contest of skill and science that is to take place there this very Friday night between a party by the name of Lefty Ledoux and another party by the name of Mickey McCoy, who are very prominent middleweights.

Now ordinarily I will not go around the corner to see a contest of skill and science between Lefty Ledoux and Mickey McCoy, or anybody else, as far as that is concerned, unless they are using blackjacks and promise to hurt each other, but I am the guest on this trip of a party by the name of Meyer Marmalade, and I will go anywhere to see anything if I am a guest.

This Meyer Marmalade is really a most superior character, who is called Meyer Marmalade because nobody can ever think of his last name, which is something like Marmalodowski, and he is known far and wide for the way he likes to make bets on any sporting proposition, such as baseball, or horse races, or ice hockey, or contests of skill and science, and especially contests of skill and science.

So he wishes to be present at this contest in Boston, Mass., between Lefty Ledoux and Mickey McCoy to have a nice wager on McCoy, as he has reliable information that McCoy's manager, a party by the name of Koons, has both judges and the referee in the satchel.

If there is one thing Meyer Marmalade dearly loves, it is to have a bet on a contest of skill and science of this nature, and so he is going to Boston, Mass. But Meyer Marmalade is such a guy as loathes and despises traveling all alone, so when he offers to pay my expenses if I will go along to keep him company, naturally I am pleased to accept, as I have nothing on of importance at the moment and, in fact, I do not have anything on of importance for the past ten years.

I warn Meyer Marmalade in advance that if he is looking to take anything off of anybody in Boston, Mass., he may as well remain at home, because everybody knows that statistics show that the percentage of anything being taken off of the citizens of Boston, Mass., is less per capita than anywhere else in the United States, especially when it comes to contests of skill and science, but Meyer Marmalade says this is the first time they ever had two judges and a referee running against the statistics, and he is very confident.

Well, by and by I go from the dining-car back to my seat in another car, where Meyer Marmalade is sitting reading a detective magazine, and I speak of seeing Joey Perhaps to him. But Meyer Marmalade does not seem greatly interested, although he says to me like this:

"Joey Perhaps, eh?" he says. "A wrong gee. A dead wrong gee. He must just get out. I run into the late Jack Ortega's brother, young Ollie, in Mindy's restaurant last week," Meyer Marmalade says, "and when we happen to get to talking of wrong gees, naturally Joey Perhaps' name comes up, and Ollie remarks he understands Joey Perhaps is about due out, and that he will be pleased to see him some day. Personally," Meyer Marmalade says, "I do not care for any part of Joey Perhaps at any price."

Now our car is loaded with guys and dolls who are going to Boston, Mass., to witness a large football game between the Harvards and the Yales at Cambridge, Mass., the next day, and the reason I know this is because they are talking of nothing else.

So this is where the football starts getting into this story.

One old guy that I figure must be a Harvard from the way he talks seems to have a party all his own, and he is getting so much attention from one and all in the party that I figure he must be a guy of some importance, because they laugh heartily at his remarks, and although I listen very carefully to everything he says he does not sound so very humorous to me.

He is a heavy-set guy with a bald head and a deep voice and anybody can see that he is such a guy as is accustomed to plenty of authority. I am wondering out loud to Meyer Marmalade who the guy can be, and Meyer Marmalade states as follows:

"Why," he says, "he is nobody but Mr. Phillips Randolph, who makes the automobiles. He is the sixth richest guy in this country," Meyer says, "or maybe it is the seventh. Anyway, he is pretty well up with the front runners. I spot his monicker on his suitcase, and then I ask the porter, to make sure. It is a great honor for us to be traveling with Mr. Phillips Randolph," Meyer says, "because of him being such a public benefactor and having so much dough, especially having so much dough."

Well, naturally everybody knows who Mr. Phillips Randolph is, and I am surprised that I do not recognize his face myself from seeing it so often in the newspapers alongside the latest model automobile his factory turns out, and I am as much pleasured up as Meyer Marmalade over being in the same car with Mr. Phillips Randolph.

He seems to be a good-natured old guy, at that, and he is having a grand time, what with talking, and laughing, and taking a dram now and then out of a bottle, and when old Crip McGonnigle comes gimping through the car selling his football souvenirs, such as red and blue feathers, and little badges, and pennants, and one thing and another, as Crip is doing around the large football games since Hickory Slim is a two-year-old, Mr. Phillips Randolph stops him and buys all of Crip's red feathers, which have a little white H on them to show they are for the Harvards.

Then Mr. Phillips Randolph distributes the feathers around among his party, and the guys and dolls stick them in their hats, or pin them on their coats, but he has quite a number of feathers left over, and about this time who comes through the car but Joey Perhaps, and Mr. Phillips Randolph steps out in the aisle and stops Joey and politely offers him a red feather, and speaks as follows:

"Will you honor us by wearing our colors?"

Well, of course Mr. Phillips Randolph is only full of good spirits, and means no harm whatever, and the guys and dolls in his party laugh heartily as if they consider his action very funny, but maybe because they laugh, and maybe because he is just naturally a hostile guy, Joey Perhaps knocks Mr. Phillips Randolph's hand down, and says like this:

"Get out of my way," Joey says. "Are you trying to make a sucker out of somebody?"

Personally, I always claim that Joey Perhaps has a right to reject the red feather, because for all I know he may prefer a blue feather, which means the Yales, but what I say is he does not need to be so impolite to an old guy such as Mr. Phillips Randolph, although of course Joey has no way of knowing at this time about Mr. Phillips Randolph having so much dough.

Anyway, Mr. Phillips Randolph stands staring at Joey as if he is greatly startled, and the chances are he is, at that, for the chances are nobody ever speaks to him in such a manner in all his life, and Joey Perhaps also stands there a minute staring back at Mr. Phillips Randolph, and finally Joey speaks as follows:

"Take a good peek," Joey Perhaps says. "Maybe you will remember me if you ever see me again."

"Yes," Mr. Phillips Randolph says, very quiet. "Maybe I will. They say I have a good memory for faces. I beg your pardon for stopping you, sir. It is all in fun, but I am sorry," he says.

Then Joey Perhaps goes on, and he does not seem to notice Meyer Marmalade and me sitting there in the car, and Mr. Phillips Randolph sits down, and his face is redder than somewhat, and all the joy is gone out of him, and out of his party, too. Personally, I am very sorry Joey Perhaps comes along, because I figure Mr. Phillips Randolph will give me one of his spare feathers, and I will consider it a wonderful keepsake.

But now there is not much more talking, and no laughing whatever in Mr. Phillips Randolph's party, and he just sits there as if he is thinking, and for all I know he may be thinking that there ought to be a law against a guy speaking so disrespectfully to a guy with all his dough as Joey Perhaps speaks to him.

Well, the contest of skill and science between Lefty Ledoux and Mickey McCoy turns out to be something of a disappointment, and, in fact, it is a stinkeroo, because there is little skill and no science whatever in it, and by the fourth round the customers are scuffling their feet, and saying throw these bums out, and making other derogatory remarks, and furthermore it seems that this Koons does not have either one of the judges, or even as much as the referee, in the satchel, and Ledoux gets the duke by unanimous vote of the officials.

So Meyer Marmalade is out a couple of C's, which is all he can wager at the ringside, because it seems that nobody in Boston, Mass., cares a cuss about who wins the contest, and Meyer is much disgusted with life, and so am I, and we go back to the Copley Plaza Hotel, where we are stopping, and sit down in the lobby to meditate on the injustice of everything.

Well, the lobby is a scene of gayety, as it seems there are a number of football dinners and dances going on in the hotel, and guys and dolls in evening clothes are all around and about, and the dolls are so young and beautiful that I get to thinking that this is not such a bad old world, after all, and even Meyer Marmalade begins taking notice.

All of a sudden, a very, very beautiful young doll who is about 40 per cent in and 60 per cent out of an evening gown walks right up to us sitting there, and holds out her hand to me, and speaks as follows:

. . . . about three-eighths of an inch of the Harvards' goal line.

"Do you remember me?"

Naturally, I do not remember her, but naturally I am not going to admit it, because it is never my policy to discourage any doll who wishes to strike up an acquaintance with me, which is what I figure this doll is trying to do; then I see that she is nobody but Doria Logan, one of the prettiest dolls that ever hits Broadway, and about the same time Meyer Marmalade also recognizes her.

Doria changes no little since last I see her, which is quite some time back, but there is no doubt the change is for the better, because she is once a very rattle-headed young doll, and now she seems older, and quieter, and even prettier than ever. Naturally, Meyer Marmalade and I are glad to see her looking so well, and we ask her how are tricks, and what is the good word, and all this and that, and finally Doria Logan states to us as follows:

"I am in great trouble," Doria says. "I am in terrible trouble, and you are the first ones I see that I can talk to about it."

Well, at this, Meyer Marmalade begins to tuck in somewhat, because he figures it is the old lug coming up, and Meyer Marmalade is not such a guy as will go for the lug from a doll unless he gets something more than a story. But I can see Doria Logan is in great earnest.

"Do you remember Joey Perhaps?" she says.

"A wrong gee," Meyer Marmalade says. "A dead wrong gee."

"I not only remember Joey Perhaps," I say, "but I see him on the train today."

"Yes," Doria says, "he is here in town. He hunts me up only a few hours ago. He is here to do me great harm. He is here to finish ruining my life."

"A wrong gee," Meyer Marmalade puts in again. "Always a 100 per cent wrong gee."

Then Doria Logan gets us to go with her to a quiet corner of the lobby, and she tells us a strange story, as follows, and also to wit:

It seems that she is once tangled up with Joey Perhaps, which is something I never know before, and neither does Meyer Marmalade, and, in fact, the news shocks us quite some. It is back in the days when she is just about sixteen and is in the chorus of Earl Carroll's Vanities, and I remember well what a standout she is for looks, to be sure.

Naturally, at sixteen, Doria is quite a chump doll, and does not know which way is south, or what time it is, which is the way all dolls at sixteen are bound to be, and she has no idea what a wrong gee Joey Perhaps is, as he is good-looking, and young, and seems very romantic, and is always speaking of love and one thing and another.

Well, the upshot of it all is the upshot of thousands of other cases since chump dolls commence coming to Broadway, and the first thing she knows, Doria Logan finds herself mixed up with a very bad character, and does not know what to do about it.

By and by, Joey Perhaps commences mistreating her no little, and finally he

tries to use her in some nefarious schemes of his, and of course everybody along
Broadway knows that most of Joey's schemes are especially nefarious, because
Joey is on the shake almost since infancy.

Well, one day Doria says to herself that if this is love, she has all she can
stand, and she hauls off and runs away from Joey Perhaps. She goes back to her
people, who live in the city of Cambridge, Mass., which is the same place where
the Harvards have their college, and she goes there because she does not know
of any other place to go.

It seems that Doria's people are poor, and Doria goes to a business school
and learns to be a stenographer, and she is working for a guy in the real estate
dodge by the name of Poopnoodle, and doing all right for herself, and in the
meantime she hears that Joey Perhaps gets sent away so she figures her troubles
are all over as far as he is concerned.

Now Doria Logan goes along quietly through life, working for Mr. Poopnoodle, and never thinking of love, or anything of a similar nature, when she meets
up with a young guy who is one of the Harvards, and who is maybe twenty-one
years old, and is quite a football player, and where Doria meets up with this
guy is in a drug store over a banana split.

Well, the young Harvard takes quite a fancy to Doria and, in fact, he is
practically on fire about her, but by this time Doria is going on twenty, and is no
longer a chump doll, and she has no wish to get tangled up in love again.

In fact, whenever she thinks of Joey Perhaps, Doria takes to hating guys in
general, but somehow she cannot seem to get up a real good hate on the young
Harvard, because, to hear her tell it, he is handsome, and noble, and has wonderful ideals.

Now as time goes on, Doria finds she is growing pale, and is losing her ap-
petite, and cannot sleep, and this worries her no little, as she is always a first-
class feeder, and finally she comes to the conclusion that what ails her is that she is
in love with the young Harvard, and can scarcely live without him, so she admits
as much to him one night when the moon is shining on the Charles River, and
everything is a dead cold setup for love.

Well, naturally, after a little offhand guzzling, which is quite permissible
under the circumstances, the young guy wishes her to name the happy day, and
Doria has half a notion to make it the following Monday, this being a Sunday
night, but then she gets to thinking about her past with Joey Perhaps, and all,
and she figures it will be bilking the young Harvard to marry him unless she has
a small talk with him first about Joey, because she is well aware that many young
guys may have some objection to wedding a doll with a skeleton in her closet,
and especially a skeleton such as Joey Perhaps.

But she is so happy she does not wish to run the chance of spoiling everything
by these narrations right away, so she keeps her trap closed about Joey, although
she promises to marry the young Harvard when he gets out of college, which
will be the following year, if he still insists, because Doria figures that by then she

will be able to break the news to him about Joey very gradually, and gently, and especially gently.

Anyway, Doria says she is bound and determined to tell him before the wedding, even if he takes the wind on her as a consequence, and personally I claim this is very considerate of Doria, because many dolls never tell before the wedding, or even after. So Doria and the young Harvard are engaged, and great happiness prevails, when, all of a sudden, in pops Joey Perhaps.

It seems that Joey learns of Doria's engagement as soon as he gets out of the state institution, and he hastens to Boston, Mass., with an inside coat pocket packed with letters that Doria writes him long ago, and also a lot of pictures they have taken together, as young guys and dolls are bound to do, and while there is nothing much out of line about these letters and pictures, put them all together they spell a terrible pain in the neck to Doria at this particular time.

"A wrong gee," Meyer Marmalade says. "But," he says, "he is only going back to his old shake-down dodge, so all you have to do is to buy him off."

Well, at this, Doria Logan laughs one of these little short dry laughs that go "hah," and says like this:

"Of course he is looking to get bought off, but," she says, "where will I get any money to buy him off? I do not have a dime of my own, and Joey is talking large figures, because he knows my fiancé's papa has plenty. He wishes me to go to my fiancé and make him get the money off his papa, or he threatens to personally deliver the letters and pictures to my fiancé's papa.

"You can see the predicament I am in," Doria says, "and you can see what my fiancé's papa will think of me if he learns I am once mixed up with a blackmailer such as Joey Perhaps.

"Besides," Doria says, "it is something besides money with Joey Perhaps, and I am not so sure he will not double-cross me even if I can pay him his price. Joey Perhaps is very angry at me. I think," she says, "if he can spoil my happiness, it will mean more to him than money."

Well, Doria states that all she can think of when she is talking to Joey Perhaps is to stall for time, and she tells Joey that, no matter what, she cannot see her fiancé until after the large football game between the Harvards and the Yales as he has to do a little football playing for the Harvards, and Joey asks her if she is going to see the game, and naturally she is.

And then Joey says he thinks he will look up a ticket speculator, and buy a ticket and attend the game himself, as he is very fond of football, and where will she be sitting, as he hopes and trusts he will be able to see something of her during the game, and this statement alarms Doria Logan no little, for who is she going with but her fiancé's papa, and a party of his friends, and she feels that there is no telling what Joey Perhaps may be up to.

She explains to Joey that she does not know exactly where she will be sitting, except that it will be on the Harvards' side of the field, but Joey is anxious for more details than this.

"In fact," Doria says, "he is most insistent, and he stands at my elbow while I call up Mr. Randolph at this very hotel, and he tells me the exact locations of our seats. Then Joey says he will endeavor to get a seat as close to me as possible, and he goes away."

"What Mr. Randolph?" Meyer says. "Which Mr. Randolph?" he says. "You do not mean Mr. Phillips Randolph, by any chance, do you?"

"Why, to be sure," Doria says. "Do you know him?"

Naturally, from now on Meyer Marmalade gazes at Doria Logan with deep respect, and so do I, although by now she is crying a little, and I am by no means in favor of crying dolls. But while she is crying, Meyer Marmalade seems to be doing some more thinking, and finally he speaks as follows:

"Kindly see if you can recall these locations you speak of."

So here is where the football game comes in once more.

Only I regret to state that personally I do not witness this game, and the reason I do not witness it is because nobody wakes me up the next day in time for me to witness it, and the way I look at it, this is all for the best, as I am scarcely a football enthusiast.

So from now on the story belongs to Meyer Marmalade, and I will tell it to you as Meyer tells it to me.

It is a most exciting game (Meyer says). The place is full of people, and there are bands playing, and much cheering, and more lovely dolls than you can shake a stick at, although I do not believe there are any lovelier present than Doria Logan.

It is a good thing she remembers the seat locations, otherwise I will never find her, but there she is surrounded by some very nice-looking people, including Mr. Phillips Randolph, and there I am two rows back of Mr. Phillips Randolph, and the ticket spec I get my seat off of says he cannot understand why everybody wishes to sit near Mr. Phillips Randolph today when there are other seats just as good, and maybe better, on the Harvards' side.

So I judge he has other calls similar to mine for this location, and a sweet price he gets for it, too, and I judge that maybe at least one call is from Joey Perhaps, as I see Joey a couple of rows on back up of where I am sitting, but off to my left on an aisle, while I am almost in a direct line with Mr. Phillips Randolph.

To show you that Joey is such a guy as attracts attention, Mr. Phillips Randolph stands up a few minutes before the game starts, peering around and about to see who is present that he knows, and all of a sudden his eyes fall on Joey Perhaps, and then Mr. Phillips Randolph proves he has a good memory for faces, to be sure, for he states as follows:

"Why," he says, "there is the chap who rebuffs me so churlishly on the train when I offer him our colors. Yes," he says, "I am sure it is the same chap."

Well, what happens in the football game is much pulling and hauling this way and that, and to and fro, between the Harvards and the Yales without a tally right down to the last five minutes of play, and then all of a sudden the Yales shove the football down to within about three eighths of an inch of the Harvards' goal line.

At this moment quite some excitement prevails. Then the next thing anybody knows, the Yales outshove the Harvards, and now the game is over, and Mr. Phillips Randolph gets up out of his seat, and I hear Mr. Phillips Randolph say like this:

"Well," he says, "the score is not so bad as it might be, and it is a wonderful game, and," he says, "we seem to make one convert to our cause, anyway, for see who is wearing our colors."

And with this he points to Joey Perhaps, who is still sitting down, with people stepping around him and over him, and he is still smiling a little smile, and Mr. Phillips Randolph seems greatly pleased to see that Joey Perhaps has a big broad crimson ribbon where he once wears his white silk muffler.

But the chances are Mr. Phillips Randolph will be greatly surprised if he knows that the crimson ribbon across Joey's bosom comes of Ollie Ortega planting a short knife in Joey's throat, or do I forget to mention before that Ollie Ortega is among those present?

I send for Ollie after I leave you last night, figuring he may love to see a nice football game. He arrives by plane this morning, and I am not wrong in my figuring. Ollie thinks the game is swell.

Well, personally, I will never forget this game, it is so exciting. Just after the tally comes off, all of a sudden, from the Yales in the stand across the field from the Harvards, comes a long-drawn-out wail that sounds so mournful it makes me feel very sad, to be sure. It starts off something like Oh-oh-oh-oh-oh, with all the Yales Oh-oh-oh-oh-oh-ing at once, and I ask a guy next to me what it is all about.

"Why," the guy says, "it is the Yales' 'Undertaker Song.' They always sing it when they have the other guy licked. I am an old Yale myself, and I will now personally sing this song for you."

And with this the guy throws back his head, and opens his mouth wide and lets out a yowl like a wolf calling to its mate.

Well, I stop the guy, and tell him it is a very lovely song, to be sure, and quite appropriate all the way around, and then I hasten away from the football game without getting a chance to say goodby to Doria, although afterwards I mail her the package of letters and pictures that Ollie gets out of Joey Perhaps' inside coat pocket during the confusion that prevails when the Yales make their tally, and I hope and trust that she will think the crimson streaks across the package are just a little touch of color in honor of the Harvards.

But the greatest thing about the football game (Meyer Marmalade says) is I win two C's off of one of the Harvards sitting near me, so I am now practically even on my trip.

TAN 3rd TO 5-2 VICTOR

by Bob Considine

An account of Swaps' Derby victory in 1955 by the most versatile of columnists, now writing for the New York World Journal Tribune.

Swaps won the seventh race at Churchill Downs today and moved himself, his trainer and jockey into seventh heaven of horsedom. For the seventh race was the $152,500 Kentucky Derby.

Like the thunderbolts that had sounded overhead as ten princes of the turf made ready for the 81st running of America's greatest horse race, the California-bred Swaps seized the lead at the break, protected it into the back stretch against the long-shot, Trim Destiny, and refused to quit when the favorite, Nashua, looked him in the eye and challenged him for the bag of gold at the finish line.

Swaps, first horse foaled in the Golden State who has won the Derby since Morvich took it all in 1922, won from Nashua by a length and a half and paid $7.60, $3.40 and $2.60.

Mormon-owned, Mormon-trained, Swaps became a benefactor of the Church of the Latter Day Saints through his victory. One-tenth of the rich purse will be given over to church work by the owner and his wife and by trainer Meshachy Tenney, all of whom have served as missionaries. Tenney sleeps in the stall next to Swaps.

Nashua, running a wobbly race down the cloud-shrouded home stretch, paid $3.00 and $2.40. Summer Tan returned $3.00 for the show. Racing Fool, part of the Cain Hoy entry, was fourth.

The weatherman shook his fist at the 100,000 in the darkened stands, and the lightning and thunder was fit to cause the sensitive animals to bolt. But nothing else mattered when the starter rang the bell and the ten of them came rocketing out of there as if they were on earth for only this moment—as, indeed, they were.

Just two minutes, one and four-fifths seconds later, Swaps plunged under the wire. Rex Ellsworth, former cowhand who runs a small but lively breeding farm at Ontario, California, was $108,400 richer. As a matter of fact, he'll get the great gold trophy and the breeders award.

Jockey Willie Shoemaker, the strong, silent boy whose fine ride deprived Eddie Arcaro of the veteran's sixth Derby triumph, will be given a check for $10,840 for steering Swaps safely home. It was 23-year-old Willie's fourth Derby appearance and first win for the champion rider of 1953 and 1954.

Swaps' victory means there will be no triple crown winner this year. The rangy chestnut son of imported Khaled, a sire once owned by the Aga Khan, is not eligible for the Belmont. He could be entered in the Preakness two weeks hence if his owner so desired, but present plans call for the fine beast to be shipped back to the coast for additional gold that abounds there. Today's win upped his short but happy life-time earnings to $236,650. His other big one was the $100,000 added Santa Anita Derby last February.

The winner's time was only two-fifths of a second behind Whirlaway's record for the mile and a quarter classic.

The field, smallest since 1948, but so classy that the people bet a record $1,677,178 on it, was off to a good start on a track that was still fast despite the rain of a few minutes before. Out of the excruciating jam at the start, Swaps stuck his quivering nostrils. The nostrils, aiming for fortune like a double-barreled shot-gun in a bank stickup, never breathed a spot of dust.

The crowd had good-naturedly or sentimentally bawled "My Old Kentucky Home" with mint julep fervor as a tune-up. Now it just bawled for its choices. The field went cloppity-clopping past the club house for the first time with Swaps on top and G. R. White's nobody, Trim Destiny, making as if he belonged there at Swaps' rump. Just a bit back was Nashua with Eddie Arcaro sitting pretty and

Part of a woman's shoe helped a lame colt win the Derby.

the owner, William Woodward, Jr., sitting in a box. Summer Tan, Mrs. John W. Galbraith's steed, made up the rest of the aloof quartet. The others didn't matter.

They went into the back stretch in that order and, half way down the long straight road, any of them looked good enough to win.

But a pole away from the beginning of the turn for home, the men left the boys. Trim Destiny deflated like a shot balloon and dropped from contention to last.

Nashua's move was met with a bellow from the great crowd. The 8-5 shot (he had been expected to go off at 4-5) was beginning to run with the sure power of a champion. He came up on Swaps, leaving third running Summer Tan four lengths back, and we now had a two-horse race.

As Swaps barreled out of the turn, he may have noted the screaming crowd for the first time. Anyway, he paused almost imperceptibly in his stride and Arcaro and Nashua were on him like twin tigers. They were together now and it was something to see. But their union was as temporary as one of Tommy Manville's. Shoemaker cranked up his arm and gave Swaps a wallop that would have floored a mule. Swaps pulled away from Nashua like a train from a station . . . slowly, resolutely and with no intention of changing his mind.

"Swoosh went Swaps," commented a philosophical Arcaro in the jockeys' shed after Governor Lawrence W. Wetherby, Col. Bill Corum and other dignitaries persuaded Swaps to take the Blanket of Roses and Mrs. Ellsworth to take the $108,400.

It seemed to sum up what Swaps did.

Dore Schary, Metro Goldwyn Mayer, Culver City, California.

Dear Dore: I have a script which should make a good movie. It's about a horse we'll call Swaps. He has a bad foot, but his trainer fixes it by adding parts of a woman's shoe to the colt's own metal shoe—and he wins the Kentucky Derby.

But that's not all. Swaps, as we'll call this animal, is owned by a couple of old cowpokes who are Mormon missionaries on the side. So is the wife of one of the owners. When they win the Derby with Swaps, the first thing they do is send a "tithe" of the $108,400 to the Church of the Latter Day Saints.

And, oh, yes, the trainer. We'll call him some biblical name, like Meshachy Tenney. He sleeps right in with Swaps. Right on the straw. And one more thing, the regular rider—we'll give him some simple name like John Barton—can't make it to the Derby. He's out on missionary work. He's a Mormon, too.

Any interest? Yours truly,

BOB CONSIDINE.

Dear Bob: Sorry, am not interested. Nobody would believe it.

Yours truly,

DORE

THEY'LL REMEMBER THIS ONE

by Bill Corum

"When in the mood, he could bring tears to the driest eye." Late columnist and president of Churchill Downs, Corum covered the greatest upset in Rose Bowl history in 1934.

GREAT FOOTBALL GAMES WILL COME AND GO, and mighty California teams will one day lead the big parade again. But out here on the majestic Pacific Coast, vaunted home of vaunted elevens and sometimes sunny days, they'll remember how a great-hearted, 4 to 1 underdog Columbia team from the sidewalks of old New York leveled mighty Stanford in the mud of the Rose Bowl on January 1, 1934.

Oh, yes, they'll remember this one. They'll remember how, not once but three times, with their cleats dug deep in those last white lines, a football team that was outnumbered, outweighed and out-manned, but not outfought, rose up and threw back one desperate Cardinal charge after the other while 35,000 looked on in wonder and dismay.

They'll remember how the black-haired, black-browed Al Barabas, the Austrian howitzer, spoke once early in the second period and, on the most perfect play of the ball game, raced seventeen yards to the only touchdown. They'll remember, too, how Newt Wilder place-kicked the extra point.

But heavy cleats only dent great hearts, they do not break them. And the "little" boys from way back East still knew how to fight and fight and keep on fighting, until at the finish it was Stanford that was thoroughly licked physically and mentally, and on its heels in a dogged retreat that might have led to another Columbia score had not the poised, confident Cliff Montgomery been content to let well enough alone.

Sure, they'll remember. How can they forget? Before the final whistle, everybody on the Stanford team, except Coach Thornhill, had played. And Tiny must have itched to throw his 200 pounds in there against the savage charges of those unbelievable kids who bent but never broke under the trip-hammer blows of Bobby Grayson and Co.

Oh, he was all the backs you've ever seen, this Grayson was on this day. Dazzlingly fast even in the slippery going, he was all but unstoppable. All but . . . but not quite. For when he finally laid it all on the line three yards from home on a heart-stopping lunge, it was Al Ciampa, a bespectacled, studious-looking, 165-pounder from Brockton High School, Brockton, Massachusetts, who picked him up and hurled him back as if he were a babe in arms.

Let me try and set the picture for you.

It was the third period. The big scoreboard, its white letters and numerals standing out in sharp relief against the gray of the day, told an amazing story. Back of the "S" there was a zero. On the other side was the "C" with its tantalizing 7. Through fleeting sunshine and shadows and gusty windblown spatters of rain, the middleweight Lions had held their heavyweight foes in check.

As one Columbia rooter had said: "The game seemed all wrong. Every time Stanford sent in a replacement, he seemed larger than the man he relieved, and every time a substitute trotted out from the Columbia bench, he seemed smaller."

But here it was the third period, and the clock was beginning to play for Columbia. Stanford, which had started confidently, nonchalantly, as befitted the

. . . for 17 yards to the only touchdown.

champions of the Pacific Coast Conference and the team that had humbled the supposedly invincible Trojans of Southern California by 13 to 7, was starting to put the pressure on. "Enough of this," the young giants in the scarlet jerseys must have been saying to themselves. "This has gone far enough!"

So, "Nephew Bobbie" Grayson ripped off 23 yards. And it was first down for Stanford on the thirteen-yard line. Grayson and Hamilton tried the by now familiar reverse for two more, and then the year's greatest back pushed through on a delayed buck for eight, and it was Stanford's ball three yards from that last stripe, and Grayson was galloping.

I suppose at that moment a betting man could have got 20 to 1 that the Indians would score. You could sense the feeling throughout the crowd huddled under its umbrellas and newspapers. The blow that would make the Lion quail was about to be delivered. Grayson would crack 'em wide apart. Captain Bill Corbus, baby-faced All-American and Phi Beta Kappa, would kick the extra point to make it a tie, and then Stanford would go on from there to show them how the game of football should be played.

As I said, the offering would have been at least 20 to 1 in that crowd, and all over California where people were listening in on the game, and with no takers. But they were reckoning without that Lion. Not even Clyde Beatty could have cowed him this day. His mane was bristling, and when Grayson hurled himself forward, something hit him amidships. I think it was a chunk of a kid named Steve Dzambe and two or three more in the Blue and White. But no great matter.

That was only one down. Three more downs to go. Give it to Grayson again! So they gave it to Grayson, and once more those driving, powerful legs of his threshed as he spun and charged. And, once more, those kids with their bellies on the ground came up with the crash and, once more, Grayson stopped as though a bullet had felled him.

So now it was third down, and they must try deception . . . or what passed for deception. They pulled the reverse Grayson to Hamilton, and this time Mr. Hamilton went down in a smother of clawing Lions and the ball was still that same three yards from home. Bad, yes. But not cause for alarm. There was one more down and Bobby wouldn't fail.

He slanted off tackle like a rocket, but Ciampa, who had just come in for Newt Wilder and whose bright, clean jersey stood out like a beacon in that low-flung line, also leaped with the snap of the ball. Ciampa's head bored into his chest and, wonder of wonders, it was Grayson who was lifted off his feet and dropped back with a sickening thud.

The loss would have been two yards, and it would have been the Lion's ball on their own five, but so fiercely had Ciampa jumped him that the ball flew out of Grayson's arms and seesawed idly toward the goal line. There was a moment of agony among the small band of Columbia rooters, and then once more Barabas filled the hero's role. He lunged, and gathered the ball into his arms.

Montgomery, who was in the thick of every attacking and defensive surge, riding through the fiercest of the going like the plume of Henry of Navarre, kicked out, but the kick was hurried and short and went only to the twenty-five. Grayson, who finally finished the game with two broken ribs as a result of Ciampa's earthquake tackle, hadn't recovered his composure, and on the first play he fumbled, Owen McDowell recovering for the men of Morningside.

This time, Monty's kick went to the forty-five. Grayson, who was just about the whole Stanford team, was not through yet. He knifed through and scooted twenty yards before Montgomery, the sole defender, nailed him with a hound's tooth tackle. This was the third time in the game that "Bullet Bob" had failed to get past "Climax Cliff" with the goal line in sight.

But just the same, Stanford was surging again. Grayson added another first down on the next play to make it six in that period for the losers against none for Columbia. Here, Columbia lost five yards for delaying the game, as Little sent in his first string with the ball on the nine-yard line. Once, twice and three times they stopped 'em again and then, on fourth down, a Stanford passer was nailed for an eight yard loss.

There the third period ended. Now the minutes were definitely ticking on the side of what had, at the outset, been counted a forlorn hope. And now the mighty Montgomery made things even brighter by booting the heavy water-soaked ball sixty yards to midfield from behind his own goal.

He's not what you would call a terrific punter, but his poise, know-how and steel-like nerve always tell in the clutches. When he has to make 'em go, he makes 'em go, and he always seemed to have the right-of-way to the coffin corner. Twice in this, his last game on any field, he missed it by inches when the kick might well have set the Cardinals down on their own one-foot line.

Grayson tried it again from there, but Ed Brominski, the blond Pole of Little's backfield, was in front of him, with one of those unerring, jarring tackles. So Alustiza had to kick, and the alarmed Stanfordites started what turned out to be a losing battle against time.

That was the game . . . and one of the greatest upsets in the history of collegiate football.

WALCOTT-CHARLES TITLE FIGHT

by James P. Dawson

The late Times *man came up with one of those rare sports stories—one in which even the loser must have been happy for the winner.*

IN A BOXING UPSET EVEN MORE STARTLING than the victory of Randy Turpin over Ray Robinson in London last week, Jersey Joe Walcott, of Camden, to-night became the oldest fighter in ring history to win the world heavyweight crown, when he knocked out Ezzard Charles in the seventh round at Forbes Field, Pittsburgh.

Under the force of a left hook to the jaw, Charles fell forward, his gloved fists under him, his nerves deadened, while the crowd of more than 28,000 came to its feet with an ear-splitting roar for the man who triumphed at 37 years of age, after four previous failures.

Referee Buck McTiernan, in unison with Tommy Grant, the knockdown timekeeper outside the ring, tolled off the fatal seconds as Charles tried unsuccessfully to lift himself off the canvas. He worked his arms fitfully, trying for leverage. At "six" he managed to raise his head. At "eight" his arms came free. At "ten" the beaten champion was halfway to standing as the referee signaled the end of the fight. Charles toppled over backwards. He was out cold.

In an emotional reaction to his amazing win, Walcott almost fainted after the ten-second count certified his victory, and the beginning of his reign as world champion. Friends and fans stormed the ring to congratulate the new ruler of the heavyweights. Police fought their way through the steaming crowd to protect him.

Walcott, breathing heavily, dropped to his knees and tried to say something over the radio. He was unable to speak. And even if he could have, he would not have been heard above the din.

Here was a man, at a time in life when the average boxer has long since retired, crowning a career that reached back through twenty-one years with a title victory that is without parallel in ring annals.

A conspicuous underdog in the betting, 6 to 1 at fight time, and deservedly so by the record, Walcott was conceded only an outside chance. As it turned out, the crowd was rewarded with a finish about which they can talk for a long time. For no fighter was ever more totally and convincingly put away then Charles.

Restored to consciousness in his corner, the defeated Ohioan was escorted,

almost unnoticed, from the ring, while the crowd showered all its attention on the emotionally stricken Walcott.

In his dressing room, Charles attributed his defeat to a lucky punch. "It was a sucker punch," he said. "Why I ever got in the way of it, I'll never know."

It was necessary to take two stitches in Charles' lower lip, and his handlers had to stanch the blood flow from a cut under his right eye, and depress a swelling under the left. Walcott was unmarked. He was a formidable opponent tonight, and Jersey Joe did not beat an inferior Charles. He battered into helplessness a fighter who was trained to the minute, lithe, powerful and sure-footed.

The Walcott of tonight did not slap and run, stab and hold. This was a cagey, alert boxer, who measured his blows carefully and landed them so frequently that he was ahead on the official ring ballots at the finish.

It was not a spectacular bout up to the seventh, which made the finish all the more exciting.

Cautious sparring characterized the first two rounds, though it had been expected that Charles, eager to get the wiley Walcott out of his life, would try to overwhelm him with a whirlwind assault from the starting bell.

Surprisingly, Charles waited for Walcott to carry the fight to him. Walcott fought shrewdly. He locked Charles' arms in the close range action.

In the third round, Walcott became bold. He dug two left hooks to Ezzard's body and followed with several stabbing lefts to the face. Sparring carefully, wasting no move, ready to strike with either hand, he bided his time as Charles pawed forward with several light lefts to the face. Suddenly, Jersey Joe hooked a left for the jaw that landed high. The blow caught Charles under the right eye, ripping the flesh. This was followed by a right to the jaw as Charles stumbled in, head down. Walcott was swift to attack, driving a left and right to the head before the end of the round.

Walcott held command thereafter.

Four solid left hooks to the head stung Charles to a fiery, explosive bit of infighting, during which he pounded Walcott savagely about the body near the end of the sixth.

They were sparring at long range in the center of the ring in the seventh when Walcott lowered the boom—a lightning-like, paralyzing left hook to the jaw. Charles went down and out, his string of victories checked at twenty-four.

And the man who had quit the ring more than once because he was unable to make a living for his large family was the new heavyweight champion of the world.

Overwhelmed with emotion, unable to speak.

ARMY BLACK AND NAVY BLUE

by Ring Lardner

He titled his autobiography, "The Story of a Wonder Man." And that he was. Possibly no American author has matched his wit. This classic was written in 1929.

AFTER AN ARMISTICE LASTING TWO YEARS the Army and Navy met in football at the Polo Grounds in New York, Saturday, and battled to one of their old-fashioned scoreless ties before a crowd that would have taxed the capacity of a station wagon and might have been even larger if people had thought Stanford was going to play Notre Dame. The stands were full of uniformed bell captains and half-dressed women who had left home in a hurry and were impatient to get back.

Only a small part of the entertainment was provided by the rival teams. Most of it was derived from the gala attire and holiday spirit of the spectators, the presence of internationally famous men, the drills and marches of the undergraduates, the music of the bands and the antics of the cheer leaders, who apparently had been studying new "stuff" to spring on this occasion. One of them almost stopped the show before it started by turning a "cartwheel"; it made such a hit with the crowd that, when the game was under way, in place of the usual cries of "Hold 'em!" and "Touchdown!" the air was rent with vague murmurs of "Cartwheel!"

The cadets from West Point were first to reach the scene. They came down the Hudson in a canoe, disembarked at the corner of the Harlem River and 155th Street and marched into the grounds headed by a two-piece band consisting of an A cornet, of which one musician carried the mouthpiece and headrest and another the valves. They stopped in front of General Pershing's empty box and sang "Old Nassau" to throw people off.

A few minutes later the "middies" arrived from Annapolis in a two-seated barracks, and immediately began kidding the cadets with such remarks as "Ah, there!" and "Skidoo!" The Army adherents replied in kind and displayed a surprising aptitude for banter. Judge Landis pounded Mrs. Landis with a gavel and explained briefly the terms of the compromise by which a resumption of football relations between the two schools had been effected. The Army, he said, had agreed not to use players who had gone to Oxford.

The West Point athletes, led by Captain Charles Daly, came through the west gate at 1:57, riding horses. When they had removed their Minnesota, Georgia Tech, Penn State and Oregon sweaters, they presented a striking appearance in buff step-ins, but the Annapolis cohorts were even more daring, dressed only in seal ring marks acquired in a game with Princeton.

Captains Daly and Dashiell were summoned to the center of the gridiron by Referee Tom Thorp, who took a quarter out of his overnight bag and bit it in two. He read the rules aloud and suggested that the periods be called chukkers as a tribute to the Polo Grounds. The captains seemed on the point of making no reply when John Brown of the Navy kicked off to Oliphant. "Ollie" ran the ball back ninety-two yards for a touchdown, but was out of bounds every step of the way

Only a small part of the entertainment was provided by the rival teams.

The Army camel and the Navy milch cow.

and the Army was penalized half the distance to West Point.

French and Hackett replaced Oliphant and Cagle, who were evidently suffering from nervousness and lack of experience. Oliphant, who had been in the insurance business, explained afterwards that just as he caught the ball he looked into the stands and recognized Mr. Coolidge by his cowboy hat, and thought this would be a good chance to meet him and swap anecdotes. Mr. Coolidge gave out a statement to the effect that he was not there to sell insurance, but as a substitute for President Hoover, who is a headliner at Keith's in Washington this week. Oliphant merely shrugged when he read this statement.

The Navy took the ball while the cadets were attending classes. A forward pass, Shapley to Lloyd, and an exhibition of tap-dancing by Barchet carried the pigskin to the West Point twelve-yard line. The midshipmen appeared to be exposed to an almost certain touchdown, but Ingram called them into a muddle and the danger was averted by Jack Dalton, who drop-kicked back to his own thirty-yard line with his left heel.

The Army returned to the field and from then until the end of the half it seemed almost impossible for one team or the other to help scoring, but as is generally the case in this classic the rival elevens showed the results of long practice hours behind closed gates and were able to keep their offense a secret.

There was plenty to amuse and entertain the crowd between halves. The Flonzaley quartet (three drums and a ukulele), dressed in naval uniforms, marched to the middle of the field and formed a gigantic letter "H" as a token of respect to President Hoover, Hindenburg, Harvard, Henry Ford, Hope Hampton, the Happiness Boys and Clara Bow.

One of the cheer leaders (not the one that turned the cartwheel) then requested that the Secretary of War and the Secretary of the Navy stand up and take a bow. The two officers complied, but refused to give their names. Eddie Cantor got fifty dollars for announcing that Rutgers would play Cornell next Saturday in secret.

A group from the cheering sections paraded the side lines leading the rival mascots: the Army camel and the Navy milch cow. Some of the boys, in fun, tried to get the animals to kiss. Much to the surprise of the ringleaders in this bit of devilment, the two mascots liked the idea.

The Army players were late in showing up for the second half as somebody had started a rumor that Pop Warner and Knute Rockne had joined the Navy. The line-ups were unchanged excepting that Cagle and Oliphant were once more in the Army backfield, having gone through Harvard and Columbia during the intermission.

Some of the athletes had unfortunately misunderstood the coaches' instructions in the dressing-rooms. The coaches had told them to do a lot of punting; they thought he had said punning. The result was morbid. For example, in the third chukker a Navy end and an Army end collided with terrific force and got mad at each other.

"You Woodruff me, would you?" said the Army man.

"I'll make you wish you'd never been Born," replied the midshipman.

A few plays later there was ill feeling between the two centers.

"I'll carry you out in a pail, Garbisch," said one.

"And while you're doing it I'll give you the razz, Perry," retorted the West-Pointer.

And still later, a Navy tackle intercepted an Army end running down the field to cover a kick.

"Where are you going, my Merrilat?"

"I'm going for a Cruise. Don't be so Flippen."

It is impossible for this writer to record any more of the dialogue.

The game was called when the two mascots minced on the field simultaneously and announced that it was milking time. A big demonstration followed, during which President Stoneham of the New York Giants tore up the goal posts and wondered why he had ever planted them.

LINE-UP

Army (0)		Navy (0)
Merrilat	l. e.	Lloyd
Timberlake	l. t.	Flippen
McEwen	l. g.	Carney
Garbisch	c.	Perry
Erwin	r. g.	Larson
Bunker	r. t.	Ralston
Born	r. e.	Gilchrist
Daly	q. b.	Dashiell
Cagle	l. h. b.	Barchet
Oliphant	r. h. b.	Roberts
Murrell	f. b.	Norton

Substitutions—Army: Tipton for Erwin; Jones for Garbisch; Mulligan for Timberlake; Devore for Mulligan; Tit for Tat; Tea for Two; Smythe for Daly; Vidal for Smythe; Hackett for Cagle; Wilson for Oliphant; French for Post no Bills. Navy: Taylor for Lloyd; Nicholls for Gilchrist; Woodruff for Nicholls; King for Ralston; Shewell for King; Murray for Shewell; Levenski for Larson; Ingram for Dashiell; Brown for Barchet; Shapley for Roberts; Dalton for Norton; Cruise for Dalton; Navy forever; Change for local. Referee—Tom Thorp. Umpire—Ed Thorp. Field Judge—Jim Thorpe. Head Linesman—Mrs. Thorpe. Shoes by Moran and Mack.

THE
UNFORGETTABLES

GAME CALLED

by Grantland Rice

*Most affectionately regarded sportsman of them all,
he pinned the tail of immortality on Notre Dame's
1922 backfield: "The Four Horsemen." This poem
in memory of Babe Ruth was written in 1948.*

*Game called by darkness—let the curtain fall,
No more remembered thunder sweeps the field.
No more the ancient echoes hear the call
To one who wore so well both sword and shield.
The Big Guy's left us with the night to face,
And there is no one who can take his place.
Game called—and silence settles on the plain.
Where is the crash of ash against the sphere?
Where is the mighty music, the refrain
That once brought joy to every waiting ear?
The Big Guy's left us, lonely in the dark,
Forever waiting for the flaming spark.
Game called—what more is there for one to say?
How dull and drab the field looks to the eye.
For one who rules it in a golden day
Has waved his cap to bid us all good-bye.
The Big Guy's gone—by land or sky or foam
May the Great Umpire call him "safe at home."*

T HE GREATEST FIGURE the world of sport has ever known has passed from the field. Game called on account of darkness. Babe Ruth is dead.

There have been mighty champions in their day and time from John L. Sullivan to Jack Dempsey—such stars as Bobby Jones, Ty Cobb, Walter Johnson, on and on, who walked along the pathway of fame.

But there has been only one Babe Ruth—one Bambino, who caught and held the love and admiration of countless millions around the world.

From the time he appeared on the big league scene with the Boston Red Sox in 1914, to the day his playing career ended more than 20 years later, Ruth was the greatest all-around ballplayer in the history of the game. He was a brilliant

132

And there is no one who can take his place.

left-handed pitcher—the top power hitter of all time—a star defensive outfielder who could be rated with the best.

He was the one ballplayer who was a master of offense and defense—the nonpareil in both.

But Ruth was something more than a great ballplayer. He was an emblem, a symbol. No other athlete ever approached his color, not even the colorful Jack Dempsey, who had more than his share.

Babe Ruth's appeal to the kids of this nation was something beyond belief. He loved them and the kids knew it. There was nothing phony about his act. The kids knew the Babe was the greatest home run hitter of all time—that he

133

was one of the greatest pitchers of all time—that he was an able place-hitter—that he could do more with a bat and a baseball than any player that ever lived. And the Babe could. But they also knew he was their pal.

I was present when he drove 60 miles one night before a world series game in Chicago to see a sick boy. "And if you write anything about it," he said, "I'll knock your brains out." He meant it that way.

Oddly enough, the Babe and Walter Johnson, the two stars on offense and defense, the mighty hitter and the whirlwind pitcher, died from the same cause —a tumor attached to the brain.

And once again, oddly enough, it was Babe Ruth who was Johnson's nemesis in the box and at the bat. He told me once that he had beaten Johnson six times by the scores of 1 to 0. And even the great Johnson was none too keen about facing him from the firing hill.

I've been a close friend of Babe Ruth since 1919, nearly 30 years ago when the Red Sox and Giants traveled north from spring training together.

The true story of Babe's life will never be written—the story of wrecked cars he left along the highway—the story of the night he came near dropping Miller Huggins off a train—the story of the $100,000 or more he lost in Cuba one racing winter. (The Babe told me it was $200,000.)

The story of the ribald, carefree Babe who ignored all traffic signals. I was riding home with Ruth one night after a game of golf. The Babe was late. He ignored red lights and everything else in a big car. I begged Babe to let me get out and take a taxi. The Babe only laughed.

"These cops are my pals," he said. "A funny thing happened yesterday. Maybe I'd had a shot or so too much. Anyway, my car stalled. A big cop came up and asked what the matter was.

" 'It won't run,' I said.

" 'You're drunk,' the cop said.

"I hit him in the nose.

" 'Now I know you're drunk, you so-and-so,' the cop said.

"He shoved me out of the way and drove me home."

One day the Babe was going the wrong way on a road to some golf club.

"Hey, this is a one-way street," some traffic cop hollered.

"I'm only driving one way, you dumb—," the Babe said.

The cop, enraged, came rushing up, "Oh, hello Babe," he said. "I didn't know it was you. Drive any way you want to."

I sat one day with Babe at St. Albans, his golf club. The Babe took out a .22 rifle, and he and a pal began shooting away the door knob at a $1 a shot. The Babe missed some guy who had just opened the door by two inches. "He should have knocked," the Babe said.

Just one day with the Babe was a big adventure. There was the time he planted a small explosive bomb in some pal's car and almost blew up the place, including the Babe and myself. "I didn't know it was that strong," was all he said.

He was a rough, rowdy, swaggering figure, more profane than anyone I ever hope to meet again, with a strong sense of decency and justice and fair play. He was a sportsman, if I ever saw one. He wanted no advantage at any start.

There was the day Miller Huggins was going to fine Ruth $5,000. He had been absent two days. The fine was to be plastered after the game. All baseball writers were notified. The Babe appeared before the game, red-eyed and dazed looking. He was in terrible shape. He hit two home runs and a triple. Huggins forgot the fine.

These are among the true stories of Babe Ruth, who had no regard for the conventions of the common or normal man, whether this included action or words. But, beyond all this, he was open-hearted, friendly, always cheerful, a great guy to be with.

I can still hear the roar of voices wherever he was. There was nothing quiet and sedate about the Babe.

He could recall few names. "I caught back of him for 10 years," Mickey Cochrane once told me. "But he never knew my name. It was 'Hello, kid.'"

Driving around, Babe always responded to those who called out, "Hey, Babe." His reply was "Hello, Mom," or "Hello, Pop."

"They can't forget my funny-looking pan," he said once. They won't forget his funny-looking pan soon. His records were terrific, but they meant little when compared to the man who was so far above all the records he ever set. I've never seen him turn a mean trick.

No game will ever see his like, his equal again. He was one in many, many lifetimes. One all alone.

POP-OFF KID

by Quentin Reynolds

War correspondent, author of The Wounded Don't Cry, *Reynolds turned his hand to a sketch of one of baseball's greatest personalities (1939).*

THERE WAS A TIME WHEN YOU COULD SHOOT DEER, grouse or penguins in the upper-tier stands at Ebbets Field, Brooklyn, but today the upper tiers are filled with Joe Doakes and his brother, raising lusty voices in praise of the Dodgers in general and one Leo Ernest Durocher in particular.

Some of this truly amazing increase in attendance can be traced to Larry McPhail, who introduced such foibles as night baseball, foot racing, bowling on the green, and goodness knows what else as adjuncts to the national pastime. Larry's motto is, "Keep the customers awake and you'll keep 'em comin'." He's done that.

However, the vermilion-thatched Mister McPhail would be the first to admit that the real reason for the record-breaking support the Dodgers are getting this year is that taut bundle of loquacity who goes by the aforementioned name of Leo Ernest Durocher, shortstop extraordinary, verbal battler par excellence and a manager who does a great deal more than just growl, "Go up and slap one."

Leo Durocher has a reputation for pugnacity second to none. It is a reputation well deserved, and it dates from the first day of his first full season with the Yankees, which was 1928. The Yanks opened in Philadelphia with the Athletics that year and Ty Cobb was playing out his string with the A's. Tony Lazzeri had hurt his arm and Huggins asked Leo if he had ever played second base.

"Sure, Hug," Leo said confidently, "I've played it more than I have shortstop."

Parenthetically it might be noted that Mr. Durocher seldom had seen second base, even via the base-hit route. So the Yanks opened with a rookie who had never played the position on second base.

Babe Ruth said to Leo, "Listen, kid, if that Cobb rides you, here's what to say to him; say, 'Listen, you penny-pinching . . .'"

The game wasn't very old before Cobb got a base hit. It was two out and Tris Speaker, also playing out his string, was at bat. He slashed a grounder between second and first. Before the ball had hit the bat Cobb was off. Durocher came in for the ball and he met it on the base path. Leo gave Cobb a gentle push with his hip. Cobb had to lose a split second and then run around him. Durocher fielded

136

"It was that Pop-off kid who licked us."

the ball, shot it to second, and Cobb was an easy out.

With cold fury Cobb turned to Durocher and said, "If you ever do that again I'll cut your legs off."

Durocher remembered his instructions from the Babe. He drew a deep breath and in a shrill voice that could be heard from here to there yelled, "Say, listen, you penny-pinching old (censored) . . ."

He went on from there. Cobb was wild, and he shouted back that he'd be waiting under the grandstand after the game. He was, too, but as he came up to make mincemeat out of Leo the huge bulk of Babe Ruth intervened.

"Look, Ty, you wouldn't hit a kid, would you?" the Babe wheedled. "Look at the size of him. He didn't know what he was saying. Now, kid, you run along to the clubhouse and get dressed."

"Me calling Ty Cobb anything was great, wasn't it?" he grins now. "He was the best there ever was and I should have called him Mr. Cobb. You see, Ty had sense enough to save his money and invest it and today he's wealthy. Some of the guys who used to call him 'penny-pincher' are looking for jobs as coaches in very minor leagues.

"It was Babe Ruth's fault. That's how he played the game, God bless him. He'd get me into an average of two fights a game, but he'd always get me out of them. He got me out of a thousand fights."

Funny thing about Leo: he wouldn't be playing ball today if it hadn't been for a big kindly Negro factory worker up in West Springfield, Massachusetts. His name was David Red.

Leo had four brothers and all of them played ball. During the early 1920's the industrial leagues in New England outdrew many organized minor leagues. Every factory had its ball club; every factory owner liked to bet on his team.

Leo was working for the Wyco Electric Company, learning to make motorcycle batteries, and of course playing shortstop for the team. One day he got a letter from Jim Clark, who managed the Hartford team, asking him to report for a tryout. Leo laughed at that. Why, Hartford was just about the best team in the world. He told big David Red about the letter and also added that he was not going.

But big David Red, who worked alongside of Leo, decided otherwise. "Listen, boy, that's your chance. Get on down there to Hartford."

"But that's a fast league," Leo protested. "Why, even Benny Traske couldn't make it. Neither could his brother Eddie, and there's the two best ballplayers I ever saw."

"Listen, boy," big David Red said, "you go to Hartford and try out like Mr. Clark says. I'm telling you, boy, you're as good as any of them. Yes suh."

Leo listened for a couple of days and then the Negro's persuasiveness won him over. He decided to go to Hartford.

That was 1925 and Leo has been playing professional baseball ever since. Hartford was a Yankee farm and at the end of the season the Yanks brought Leo down to look him over.

He was the freshest rookie ever to come up to the big show, and he was with one of the toughest of all clubs. Ruth and Meusel and Aaron Ward and Joe Dugan were always ready to throw a punch at almost anyone. Those Yankees had just won the 1927 pennant and had climaxed it by murdering the Pirates in four straight games. This was a rough, hell-bent-for-leather club and Durocher fitted in fine.

At first the players, who didn't like rookies much, didn't like Durocher, but after the opening games when he put the blast on Cobb and after Ruth had put his stamp of approval on the kid he was in.

"I was lucky to break in under Hug," Leo says now. "A lot of people thought that the players ran Hug. That wasn't true. We all felt pretty bad when Hug went. We were playing on a raw, cold day in 1929. I went into the locker room between games. Hug was standing there in front of a mirror looking worried and fingering a sore spot on his cheek.

"He said, 'I don't feel very well,' and the way he said it scared me. I said, 'Go on home, Hug, we'll win this next one without you.' So Hug went home and a few days later he was dead. We missed Hug a lot. Me especially. Hell, he made a ballplayer out of me. In his quiet way he could teach you more than almost anyone. Hug made you play better than you knew how."

That winter Leo had a run-in with Ed Barrow, who didn't like pop-off kids much. Leo didn't like the contract that was offered him and he told Barrow. Barrow told him, "Take it or leave it."

Leo said, "I'll leave it," and then he slammed the door of Barrow's office —hard.

Barrow had him waived out of the league in about two minutes. Before Leo knew what was happening he was the property of the Cincinnati Club, and he played there until 1933 when he went to St. Louis.

There was a gang to Leo's liking. It was a whole team of pop-off kids. Frank Frisch was manager then and he was never quiet. Pepper Martin was always ready for a fight or a frolic.

The 1934 world series is one that won't be forgotten for a long time. When it was all over and the Cards had beaten Detroit in seven games, Manager Mickey Cochrane said with disgust: "It was that pop-off kid who licked us. We never thought he could hit."

Leo, of course, fielded beautifully. By now he was recognized as the best fielding shortstop in baseball. But he hit. He hit .259 for the series and he reserved his hits for important spots. The Deans and the Medwicks got the headlines, but the players gave Leo the credit.

In 1937 he went to Brooklyn for Jimmy Bucher, Johnny Cooney, Roy Henshaw and Joe Stripp, and the fans said that the Brooklyn officials were out of their minds. Leo was along in years as ballplayers went; he couldn't hit the side of an elephant with a banjo and, besides, he was always fighting. That was all true, but Leo proceeded to have his best year.

When September rolled around, everyone knew that Burleigh Grimes was going to lose his job as manager. Burleigh was a good manager, but he had committed the unpardonable sin: his team had finished in seventh place. Grimes went to Leo one day and said: "Leo, you'd like to be manager of this club. Go and put your bid in for the job."

"I'm working for you, Burleigh," Leo said shortly.

"I'm out anyway," Grimes said, "and I've recommended you for the job. Better see McPhail right away."

. . . an average of two fights a game.

Leo gulped and hurried to see Boss McPhail. McPhail was counting on Leo for his 1939 shortstop.

Leo said bluntly, "I want a chance to manage this club."

"How do you know you can do it?" McPhail said. "How do you know whether you can handle men?"

"I don't know," Leo said calmly, "but I want a chance."

Much to the surprise of everyone, including McPhail, Durocher was made manager of the Dodgers. He has shown that he can handle fractious, temperamental laddies like Van Mungo and Red Evans. And he hasn't lost anything of his colorful character.

There was that time in Cincinnati, in June. Lee Grissom, who is something of a pop-off kid himself, started to ride Leo, something an older and wiser head would never think of doing.

"You came down sick yesterday when I was working," Grissom yelled over to the Brooklyn dugout before the game. "I guess you didn't want to bat against me."

Durocher popped out of the dugout and hustled over to the Reds' bench. Then he tossed a verbal blast at Grissom that took up his character, his antecedents, his looks, ability and anatomical peculiarities. Even the hardened Cincinnati burghers in the stands looked their admiration. Leo was going great—and loud.

Grissom, nonplused, could only snarl: "You'll be battin' against me one of these days. Don't forget I'm pretty fast."

Leo shouted: "I could hit you with a fungo bat, you wart-eared (censored). If I didn't want to hurt my hands I'd slug you right now, you (censored). And if you ever throw one at my head I won't duck. With that stuff you throw I won't have to duck."

One of Durocher's later exploits made every sports page in the country and precipitated a state of near-armed warfare between the Dodgers and the Giants. This one started when Bonura, deciding that Leo had tried to spike him, fired the ball at Durocher's head. Durocher countered with a stiff punch in the nose, and the riot was on. Incidentally, Bonura paid a $50 fine, but Leo was assessed only $25, leaving him with at least a financial victory.

Brooklyn had a bad time of it on the first western trip this year. Leo didn't think his team was putting it all out. After the sixth straight shellacking, which occurred in St. Louis, he went into the clubhouse and bolted the door. He wouldn't even let the players have their showers first. He set them down and I have it on the word of one of the players who was there that Leo spoke something like this:

"Listen, you bums, don't you like playing in the major leagues? Do you want to go back to the sticks? Me, I like living in good hotels and eating good and getting a good check twice a month and I'm going to fight like hell to stay up here. I'm not going to have a bunch of addled-brained clumsy nitwits like you drive me out.

"If you lose another game because of your dumbness you've got a surprise coming. I'll ship you off this team and out of the major leagues so quick you won't know what hit you. Now let me take each one of you in turn and tell you what I think of you . . ."

They started to play ball after that. Within two weeks they were in third place. And on paper the Dodgers are not a first-division team.

"What is the secret of managing a ball club?" Durocher laughed when I asked him that. "You got to know your men and handle each one differently. Take Dolph Camilli. He's the best first baseman in the league. I say to Dolph, 'You know what to do as well as I do.' That's all I say to Dolph. I know he'll be in there playing brilliantly every minute.

"Van Mungo is a great pitcher but sometimes he forgets it. I got to remind him. Red Evans? I have to pin his ears back now and then, but he's going to wind up a great pitcher. He likes beer, and once I caught him lapping it up. I bawled hell out of him and fined him a hundred dollars. He promised never to take another drink while he was with my club.

"So two weeks later in Boston I catch him in one of those merry-go-round bars, but he says very solemnly, 'Leo, I promise never to drink another beer. And this time I mean it. The nerve of those guys, charging thirty-five cents for a glass of beer!' So what could I do? I bust out laughing. Secrets of managing? There's no such thing. Get a lot of good ballplayers together, make them hustle all the time and the percentage is bound to be with you."

That's Leo Durocher, manager. Brooklyn loves him and loves his team. The Daffiness Boys have gone and today the Dodgers are an alert, bristly, fighting outfit, playing better than they know how.

FAREWELL TO THE BABE

by Paul Gallico

Stevedore, librarian, oarsman, Metropolitan Opera usher, sports editor, fiction and screenplay writer—that, in brief, is the man who eulogized Babe Didrikson in 1956.

I T IS NOW CLOSE TO TWENTY-FIVE YEARS since I first laid eyes on Babe Didrikson in the lobby of the Chapman Park Hotel in Los Angeles upon the occasion of the 1932 Olympic Games. She was then a rawhide kid of 18 with short-cut, sand-colored hair, a well-defined Adam's apple and a faint down on her upper lip. I watched her "up" to a big girl who was wearing the jacket of an Olympic competitor, pin her with her gray-green eyes and announce levelly— "Ah'm gonna whup yo' tomorrow."

We sportswriters thought that this was cockiness. There was no way for us to know at the time that it was just a simple declarative sentence spoken by a simple declarative person. It took all of us some time to find out that this lithe girl from Port Arthur, Texas who was apparently not made like other girls of sugar and spice, but instead, of whipcord, steel springs and Monel metal, enclosing the heart of a lioness, had also the makings of an extraordinary woman.

None of us who watched this unknown and unheralded youngster foresaw that she would become the greatest woman golfer that ever lived, a champion of champions, and then thrill a nation with the courage and gallantry of her battle against cancer.

There were many sports in which the Babe excelled superlatively—*all* track and field events, basketball and golf—but there was hardly any game at which she could not perform creditably, or at which she could not have become a champion, and these included swimming, diving, billiards, lacrosse, bowling and tennis. But she also invaded the men's fields. Her record for throwing a baseball still stands. She could pitch, hit and cover a bag. She could peg a football and kick left-footed. Once she even thought of boxing. Nothing came of it, but it is recorded that when she threw a punch it wasn't a roundhouse or a fly-swatter like a woman, but straight down the old trolley wire a la Ruby Goldstein, a sharpshooter of our era.

While it is true that none of the Babe's track and field or Olympic records, with the exception of the baseball throw, are still on the books today, no girl before or since has matched her record of events won in a diversity of sports.

Nor had any other woman even approached her in the number and caliber of golf championships captured, some of them played while suffering from pain, illness and physical handicaps that would have seen most grown men laid up in the hospital.

Competitively, the record she brought to Los Angeles in 1932 has never been equaled. I refer to her performance on July 16, 1932 at the National Women's AAU Track and Field Championships and Olympic tryouts at Evanston, Illinois, in which she was entered by herself as a one-woman team representing the Employers Casualty Company, of Dallas, Texas.

Singlehanded the Babe won the *team title* with an aggregate of 30 points. In second place was the famous Illinois Woman's AC, with 22 points, collected by a full complement of girls.

Now consider that in such comprehensive competitions as pentathlons or decathlons, the entrants usually excel in one or two events, are good in several more and do the best they can in the others. Thus there is a balance and the battle tends to even out. But in this incomparable performance, the girl, barely turned 18, was pitted against the best *specialists* in the entire country in *each* event, never less than half a dozen of them and sometimes two and three from one team.

On that day the Babe staged and won a private octathlon. She entered eight of the 10 events scheduled. Five of these, the 80-meter hurdles, the baseball throw, the shotput, the broad jump and the javelin toss she won outright; and in the high jump, although she equaled the world record jump of winner Jean Shiley, she was just nosed out of a tie. She placed fourth in the discus throw, picking up another point. During the course of the afternoon she set three world's records and was shut out only in the 100-meter dash, when she was just nipped in the semifinal heat.

I cannot think of any male athlete with the possible exception of old Jim Thorpe who has come even close to spread-eagling a track meet all by himself in this manner.

Two weeks later the Babe went to the Olympics in Los Angeles. Allowed to participate in only three events, against the best women of every nation, she won two of them, setting world's records in each, the javelin throw and the 80-meter hurdles. She was languaged out of the third, the high jump. After she tied with Jean Shiley for first place, at a world-record height, Babe cleared the bar in the jump-off but was ruled to have dived over. Thus she lost the record and the event. The roll that she used, incidentally, is legal today.

But prior to these events this wonderful little girl, the sixth child born to a poor Norwegian cabinetmaker and his wife who emigrated to Port Arthur, Texas, later moving to Beaumont, had already been a star basketball player named three times on the women's All-America team, a high scorer who in one game is recorded to have tanked the ball for an individual total of 106 points. And she was likewise a home run hitting star in soft ball, a crackerjack

Singlehandedly won the Women's National AAU Track and Field championships and the Olympic tryouts: Didrikson, 30 points; Illinois Women's AC, 22 points.

at pool and billiards and good enough at swimming and high diving to appear in exhibitions.

All this, however, was only the beginning of a career that was to take her to an alltime record as a golf champion, including the distinction of becoming the first American girl to break the jinx and win the British Women's Amateur championship.

Much has been made of Mrs. Zaharias' natural aptitude and talent for sports, as well as her competitive spirit and indomitable will to win, with both of which she was endowed in full measure. But not nearly enough has been said or written about the patience and strength of character expressed in her willingness to practice for endless hours, and her recognition even as a child that with all her natural ability she could reach the top and stay there only by means of incessant drill and hard work.

The hours of practice the Babe devoted in her life to various games ought to be made compulsory reading for every fresh kid who can swim, skate, run, ski a little or is handy at sports and thinks that all he or she needs to do is get out there and the opposition will swoon away. When the Babe leveled on a sister athlete and husked, "Ah'm gonna whup yo'" it wasn't brag (though an element of games-womanship and psychological attack was involved). She had put in the necessary hours of slavery to perfect her form and to be able to deliver the goods; and she just knew she could.

At 16, preparing for her first track and field meet, she would work two hours in the afternoon with her teammates and then go out alone after supper and practice from two to three hours more until darkness enveloped her, working on her step-timing for the jumps, her balance in the weight events and her starts in the sprints.

She learned golf the same way. The first full game she ever played followed the 1932 Olympics when she paired with Grantland Rice against Olin Dutra and the writer at Brentwood. She had a fine natural swing and could paste the ball as far as a man, but that isn't golf and the Babe knew it. When she decided to go in for the game seriously, she took lessons, drilled and practiced for hours on end until her hands were a mass of blisters. She taped and bandaged them and kept on, stopping only when the bandages became soaked with blood.

In the spring of 1935 while she was working for her old friends, the Employers Casualty Company in Dallas, this was her schedule:

Up at 5 in the morning and practice from 5:30 to 8:30. Report at the office at 9. During the lunch hour, putt on the carpet in the boss's office and chip balls into his leather chair. After work, back to the golf course hitting balls until dark. Thus it went, until the pain in her hands made another shot impossible. At night she would go to bed with the rule book.

It was the same story when in 1940 Babe took up tennis during the probationary period in which she was regaining her amateur golf status. Married by then to George Zaharias and living in California, she took lessons, played matches and practiced against a backboard from morning until night, for a year and a half. Had she continued, nothing could have kept her from the national championships.

But entangled as she was in the flypaper of the most ridiculous set of amateur rules ever devised, Babe quit tennis when the sportsmen running the game advised her that because she had been ruled a pro in golf she was likewise a pro in tennis. So she devoted the same long hours to bowling and became good enough to bowl major league teams in California.

Golf, however, was where Babe Didrikson reached her greatest heights. Who will ever duplicate her most impossible feat of winning 17 major golf tournaments in a row, including the National Women's Amateur, Tam O'Shanter All-American, North and South, Augusta Titleholder tourney, Broadmoor, Texas Women's Open, and finishing the sweep by capturing the British Women's Amateur championship? Only a golfer who has known the agonizing treachery of which his nerves and body are capable in letting him down in tight corners can appreciate the accumulative tension of extending a winning string of tournaments of match play against the best girl and woman golfers culled from a nation of over 143 million people and crowning this achievement by winning the one that had defied American girls for close to half a century.

Nor must it be forgotten that when the Babe had finished this grueling struggle, she was the darling of the Scots and Britons in the gallery, as well as the pet of the whole village of Gullane. She not only beat the best they had; she made them love her.

"Ah'm gonna whup yo' tomorrow."

And this is perhaps the clue as to why it may be another 50 or 75 years before such a performer as Mildred Didrikson Zaharias again enters the lists. For even if some yet unborn games queen matches her talent, versatility, skill, patience and will to practice, along with her flaming competitive spirit, and manages, let us say, to run an unbroken string of tournament victories in her specialty to 20, there still remains the little matter of courage and character, and in these departments the Babe must be listed with the champions of all times.

Indeed her unique quality has been noted, for in addition to being chosen Woman Athlete of the Year by the Associated Press poll of sportswriters and broadcasters for the years 1932, 1945, 1946, 1947 and 1950, she was named the woman athlete of the half century.

In 1953 Mildred Zaharias was stricken with cancer and suffered one of the most dangerous and excruciating of all operations, a colostomy. Yet just three and a half months after the operation, this incredibly brave and unquenchable girl was back on a golf course again in competition in the Tam O'Shanter All-American championship in killing midsummer heat in Chicago.

She did not win it. The miracle was that she fought her way back that far. Her presence on that first tee was an act of heroism that should have been rewarded with the Congressional Medal of Honor. The value of her example in inspiration to others, and the magnificence of the banner she waved aloft to those of less courage and steadfastness, cannot be overestimated.

Ten months after her operation, the Babe won the Serbin Tournament in Florida, and that same year, 1954, took the National Women's Open and this time, the Tam O'Shanter "All-American" too.

The following year all of her splendid courage was called upon again. The trouble was that she had too much of it. No longer the wiry rawhide tomboy of 18 who could practice and compete all day and dance all night, Babe was now a mature woman of 41 who had never spared herself. On a car trip vacation with two girl friends on the Texas coast she ruptured a disk in her spinal column getting the car out of sand when it got stuck. In agony with the pain in her back, she played in three more tournaments, winning one at Spartanburg, South Carolina before she was finally forced into the hospital for an operation on the ruptured disk.

Hospitalized again late in 1955 for a recurrence of cancer, her fiery fighting spirit remained undimmed and the golf clubs still accompanied her. During her first operation and again for her second they stood in the corner of her room where she could see them, play mentally over old courses, plan to correct old mistakes. They were her beloved tools, and they will forever be with her. Without them she would surely be remembered, but with them she carved herself an imperishable niche in the great American world of sports, and likewise in the hearts of all who loved her for what she was, a splendid woman.

FIGHT TO LIVE

by Al Stump

This article, written in 1961, was described by Bob Considine as "perhaps the best sports piece I have ever read."

Ever since sundown the Nevada intermountain radio had been crackling warnings: "Route 50 now highly dangerous. Motorists stay off. Repeat: AVOID ROUTE 50."

By 1 in the morning the 21-mile, steep-pitched passage from Lake Tahoe's 7,000 feet into Carson City, a snaky grade most of the way, was snow-struck, ice-sheeted, thick with rock slides and declared unfit for all transport vehicles by the State Highway Patrol.

Such news was right down Ty Cobb's alley. Anything that smacked of the impossible brought an unholy gleam to his eye. The gleam had been there in 1959 when a series of lawyers advised Cobb that he stood no chance against the Sovereign State of California in a dispute over income taxes, whereupon he bellowed defiance and sued the commonwealth for $60,000 and damages. It had been there more recently when doctors warned that liquor will kill him. From a pint of whisky per day he upped his consumption to a quart and more.

Sticking out his chin, he told me, "I think we'll take a little run into town tonight."

A blizzard rattled the windows of Cobb's luxurious hunting lodge on the crest of Lake Tahoe, but to forbid him anything—even at the age of 73—was to tell an ancient tiger not to snarl. Cobb was both the greatest of all ballplayers and a multimillionaire whose monthly income from stock dividends, rents and interests ran to $12,000. And he was a man contemptuous, all his life, of any law other than his own.

"We'll drive in," he announced, "and shoot some craps, see a show and say hello to Joe DiMaggio—he's in Reno at the Riverside Hotel."

I looked at him and felt a chill. Cobb, sitting there haggard and unshaven in his pajamas and a fuzzy old green bathrobe at 1 o'clock in the morning, wasn't fooling.

"Let's not," I said. "You shouldn't be anywhere tonight but in bed."

"Don't argue with me!" he barked. "There are fee-simple sonsofbitches all over the country who've tried it and wish they hadn't." He glared at me, flaring the

149

whites of his eyes the way he'd done for 24 years to quaking pitchers, basemen, umpires and fans.

"If you and I are going to get along," he went on ominously, *"don't increase my tension."*

We were alone in his isolated 10-room $75,000 lodge, having arrived six days earlier, loaded with a large smoked ham, a 20-pound turkey, a case of Scotch and another of champagne, for purposes of collaborating on Ty's book-length autobiography—a book which he'd refused to write for 30 years, but then suddenly decided to place on record before he died. In almost a week's time we hadn't accomplished 30 minutes of work.

The reason: Cobb didn't need a risky auto trip into Reno, but immediate hospitalization, and by the emergency-door entrance. He was desperately ill and had been even before we'd left California.

We had traveled 250 miles to Tahoe in Cobb's black Imperial limousine, carrying with us a virtual drugstore of medicines. These included Digoxin (for his leaky heart), Darvon (for his aching back), Tace (for a recently-operated-upon malignancy for the pelvic area), Fleet's compound (for his infected bowels), Librium (for his "tension"—that is, his violent rages), codeine (for his pain) and an insulin needle-and-syringe kit (for his diabetes), among a dozen other panaceas which he'd substituted for doctors. Cobb despised the medical profession.

At the same time, his sense of balance was almost gone. He tottered about the lodge, moving from place to place by grasping the furniture. On any public street, he couldn't navigate 20 feet without clutching my shoulder, leaning most of his 208 pounds upon me and shuffling along at a spraddle-legged gait. His bowels wouldn't work: they impacted, repeatedly, an almost total stoppage which brought moans of agony from Cobb when he sought relief. He was feverish, with no one at his Tahoe hideaway but the two of us to treat this dangerous condition.

Everything that hurts had caught up with his big, gaunt body at once and he stuffed himself with pink, green, orange, yellow and purple pills—guessing at the amounts, often, since labels had peeled off many of the bottles. But he wouldn't hear of hospitalizing himself.

"The hacksaw artists have taken $50,000 from me," he said, "and they'll get no more." He spoke of "a quack" who'd treated him a few years earlier. "The joker got funny and said he found urine in my whisky. I fired him."

His diabetes required a precise food-insulin balance. Cobb's needle wouldn't work. He'd misplaced the directions for the needed daily insulin dosage and his hands shook uncontrolably when he went to plunge the needle into a stomach vein. He spilled more of the stuff than he injected.

He'd been warned by experts from Johns Hopkins to California's Scripps Clinic—that liquor was deadly. Tyrus snorted and began each day with several gin-and-orange-juices, then switched to Old Rarity Scotch, which held him until night hours, when sleep was impossible, and he tossed down cognac, champagne or "Cobb Cocktails"—Southern Comfort stirred into hot water and honey.

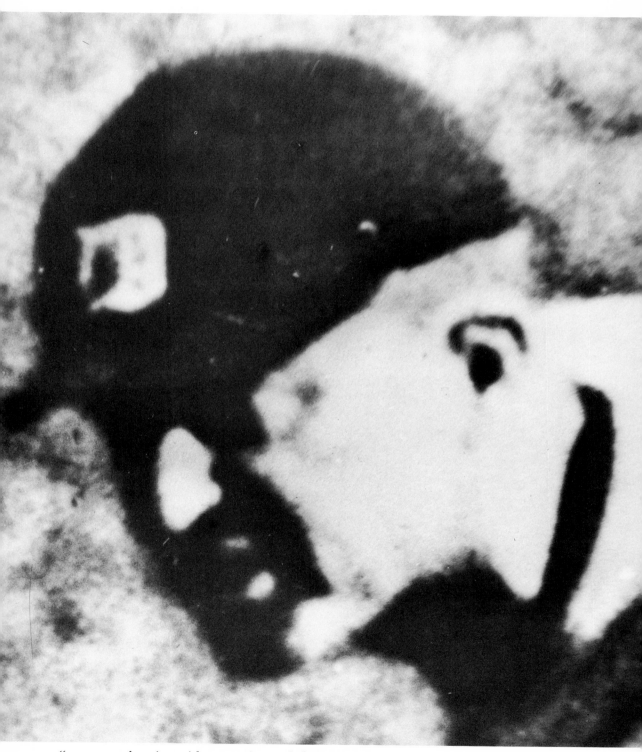

*". . . a steel spring with a growing and dangerous flaw in it
. . . if wound too tight . . . the spring will fly apart, and then it is done for."*

A careful diet was essential. Cobb wouldn't eat. The lodge was without a cook or manservant—since, in the previous six months, he had fired two cooks, a male nurse and a handyman in fits of anger—and any food I prepared for him he pushed away. As of the night of the blizzard, the failing, splenetic old king of ballplayers hadn't touched food in three days, existing solely on quarts of booze and booze mixtures.

My reluctance to prepare the car for the Reno trip burned him up. He beat his fists on the arms of his easy chair. "I'll go alone!" he threatened.

It was certain he'd try it. The storm had worsened, but once Cobb set his mind on an idea, nothing could change it. Beyond that I'd already found that to oppose or annoy him was to risk a violent explosion. An event of a week earlier had proved *that* point. It was then I discovered that he carried a loaded Luger wherever he went and looked for opportunities to use it.

En route to Lake Tahoe, we'd stopped overnight at a motel near Hangtown, California. During the night a party of drunks made a loud commotion in the parking lot. In my room next to Cobb's, I heard him cursing and then his voice, booming out the window.

"Get out of here, you —— heads!"

The drunks replied in kind. Then everyone in the motel had his teeth jolted.

Groping his way to the door, Tyrus the Terrible fired three shots into the dark that resounded like cannon claps. There were screams and yells. Reaching my door, I saw the drunks climbing each other's backs in their rush to flee. The frightened motel manager, and others, arrived. Before anyone could think of calling the police, the manager was cut down by the most caustic tongue ever heard in a baseball clubhouse.

"What kind of a pest house is this?" roared Cobb. "Who gave you a license, you mugwump? Get the hell out of here and see that I'm not disturbed! I'm a sick man and I want it quiet!"

"B-b-beg your pardon, Mr. Cobb," the manager said feebly. He apparently felt so honored to have baseball's greatest figure as a customer that no police were called. When we drove away the next morning, a crowd gathered and stood gawking with open mouths.

Down the highway, with me driving, Cobb checked the Luger and reloaded its nine-shell clip. "Two of those shots were in the air," he remarked. "The *third* kicked up gravel. I've got permits for this gun from governors of three states. I'm an honorary deputy sheriff of California and a Texas Ranger. So we won't be getting any complaints."

He saw nothing strange in his behavior. Ty Cobb's rest had been disturbed —therefore he had every right to shoot up the neighborhood.

About then I began to develop a twitch of the nerves, which grew worse with time. In past years, I'd heard reports of Cobb's weird and violent ways, without giving them much credence. But until early 1960 my own experience with the legendary Georgian had been slight, amounting only to meetings in

Scottsdale, Arizona, and New York to discuss book-writing arrangements and to sign the contract.

Locker-room stories of Ty's eccentricities, wild temper, ego and miserliness sounded like the usual scandalmongering you get in sports. I'd heard that Cobb had flattened a heckler in San Francisco's Domino Club with one punch; had been sued by Elbie Felts, an ex-Coast League player, after assaulting Felts; that he booby-trapped his Spanish villa at Atherton, California, with high-voltage wires; that he'd walloped one of his ex-wives; that he'd been jailed in Placerville, California, at the age of 68 for speeding, abusing a traffic cop and then inviting the judge to return to law school at his, Cobb's, expense.

I passed these things off. The one and only Ty Cobb was to write his memoirs and I felt highly honored to be named his collaborator.

As the poet Cowper reflected, "The innocents are gay." I was eager to start. Then—a few weeks before book work began—I was taken aside and tipped off by an in-law of Cobb's and one of Cobb's former teammates with the Detroit Tigers that I hadn't heard the half of it. "Back out of this book deal," they urged. "You'll never finish it and you might get hurt."

They went on: "Nobody can live with Ty. Nobody ever has. That includes two wives who left him, butlers, housekeepers, chauffeurs, nurses and a few mistresses. He drove off all his friends long ago. Max Fleischmann, the yeast-cake heir, was a pal of Ty's until the night a houseguest of Fleischmann's made a re-mark about Cobb spiking other players when he ran the bases. The man only asked if it was true. Cobb knocked the guy into a fish pond and after that Max never spoke to him again. Another time, a member of Cobb's family crossed him —a woman, mind you. He broke her nose with a ball bat.

"Do you know about the butcher? Ty didn't like some meat he bought. In the fight, he broke up the butcher shop. Had to settle $1,500 on the butcher out of court."

"But I'm dealing with him strictly on business," I said.

"So was the butcher," replied my informants. "In baseball, a few of us who really knew him well realized that he was wrong in the head—unbalanced. He played like a demon and had everybody hating him because he *was* a demon. That's how he set all those records that nobody has come close to since 1928. It's why he was always in a brawl, on the field, in the clubhouse, behind the stands and in the stands. The public's never known it, but Cobb's always been off the beam where other people are concerned. Sure, he made millions in the stock market—but that's only cold business. He carried a gun in the big league and scared hell out of us. He's mean, tricky and dangerous. Look out that he doesn't blow up some night and clip you with a bottle. He specializes in throwing bottles.

"Now that he's sick he's worse than ever. And you've signed up to stay with him for months. You poor sap."

Taken aback, but still skeptical, I launched the job—with my first task to drive Cobb to his Lake Tahoe retreat, where, he declared, we could work uninterrupted.

As indicated, nothing went right from the start. The Hangtown gunplay incident was an eye-opener. Next came a series of events, such as Cobb's determination to set forth in a blizzard to Reno, which were too strange to explain away. Everything had to suit his pleasure or he had a tantrum. He prowled about the lodge at night, suspecting trespassers, with the Luger in hand. I slept with one eye open, ready to move fast if necessary.

At 1 o'clock of the morning of the storm, full of pain and 90-proof, he took out the Luger, letting it casually rest between his knees. I had continued to object to a Reno excursion in such weather.

He looked at me with tight fury and said, biting out the words:

"In 1912—and you can write this down—I killed a man in Detroit. He and two other hoodlums jumped me on the street early one morning with a knife. I was carrying something that came in handy in my early days—a Belgian-made pistol with a heavy raised sight at the barrel end.

"Well, the damned gun wouldn't fire and they cut me up the back."

Making notes as fast as he talked, I asked, "Where in the back?"

"WELL, DAMMIT ALL TO HELL, IF YOU DON'T BELIEVE ME, COME AND LOOK!" Cobb flared, jerking up his shirt. When I protested that I believed him implicitly, only wanted a story detail, he picked up a half-full whisky glass and smashed it against the brick fireplace. So I gingerly took a look. A faint whitish scar ran about five inches up the lower left back.

"Satisfied?" jeered Cobb.

He described how after a battle, the men fled before his fists.

"What with you wounded and the odds 3-1," I said, "that must have been a relief."

"Relief? Do you think they could pull that on *me*? I WENT AFTER THEM!"

Where anyone else would have felt lucky to be out of it, Cobb chased one of the mugs into a dead-end alley. "I used that gunsight to rip and slash and tear him for about 10 minutes until he had no face left," related Ty, with relish. "Left him there, not breathing, in his own rotten blood."

"What was the situation—where were you going when it happened?"

"To catch a train to a ball game."

"You saw a doctor, instead?"

"I DID NOTHING OF THE SORT, DAMMIT! I PLAYED THE NEXT DAY AND GOT TWO HITS IN THREE TIMES UP!"

Records I later inspected bore out every word of it: on June 3, 1912, in a bloodsoaked, makeshift bandage, Ty Cobb hit a double and triple for Detroit, and only then was treated for the knife wound. He was that kind of ballplayer through a record 3,033 games. No other player burned with Cobb's flame. Boze Bulger, a great oldtime baseball critic, said, "He was possessed by the Furies."

Finishing his tale, Cobb looked me straight in the eye.

"You're driving me into Reno tonight," he said softly. The Luger was in his hand.

Even before I opened my mouth, Cobb knew he'd won. He had a sixth sense about the emotions he produced in others: in this case, fear. As far as I could see (lacking expert diagnosis and as a layman understands the symptoms), he wasn't merely erratic and trigger-tempered, but suffering from megalomania, or acute self-worship; delusions of persecution; and more than a touch of dipsomania.

Although I'm not proud of it, he scared hell out of me most of the time I was around him.

And now he gave me the first smile of our association. "As long as you don't aggravate my tension," he said, "we'll get along."

Before describing the Reno expedition, I would like to say in this frank view of a mighty man that the greatest, and strangest, of all American sport figures had his good side, which he tried to conceal. During the final ten months of his life I was his one constant companion. Eventually, I put him to bed, prepared his insulin, picked him up when he fell down, warded off irate taxi drivers, bartenders, waiters, clerks and private citizens whom Cobb was inclined to punch, cooked what food he could digest, drew his bath, got drunk with him and knelt with him in prayer on black nights when he knew death was near. I ducked a few bottles he threw, too.

I think, because he forced upon me a confession of his most private thoughts, that I know the answer to the central, overriding secret of his life: was Ty Cobb psychotic throughout his baseball career?

Kids, dogs and sick people flocked to him and he returned their instinctive liking. Money was his idol, but from his $4 million fortune he assigned large sums to create the Cobb Educational Foundation, which financed hundreds of needy youngsters through college. He built and endowed a first-class hospital for the poor of his backwater home town, Royston, Georgia. When Ty's spinster sister, Florence, was crippled, he tenderly cared for her until her last days. The widow of a onetime American League batting champion would have lived in want but for Ty's steady money support. A Hall of Fame member, beaned by a pitched ball and enfeebled, came under Cobb's wing for years. Regularly he mailed dozens of anonymous checks to indigent old ballplayers (relayed by a third party)—a rare act among retired tycoons in other lines of business.

If you believe such acts didn't come hard for Cobb, guess again: he was the world's champion pinchpenny.

Some 150 fan letters reached him each month, requesting his autograph. Many letters enclosed return-mail stamps. Cobb used the stamps for his own outgoing mail. The fan letters he burned.

"Saves on firewood," he'd mutter.

In December of 1960, Ty hired a one-armed "gentleman's gentleman" named Brownie. Although constantly criticized, poor Brownie worked hard as cook and butler. But when he mixed up the grocery order one day, he was fired with a check for a week's pay—$45—and sent packing.

Came the middle of that night and Cobb awakened me.

"We're driving into town *right now,*" he stated, "to stop payment on Brownie's check. The bastard talked back to me when I discharged him. He'll get no more of my money."

All remonstrations were futile. There was no phone, so we had to drive the 20 miles from Cobb's Tahoe lodge into Carson City, where he woke up the president of the First National Bank of Nevada and arranged for a stop-pay on the piddling check. The president tried to conceal his anger—Cobb was a big depositor in his bank.

"Yes, sir, Ty," he said. "I'll take care of it first thing in the morning."

"You goddamn well better," snorted Cobb. And then we drove through the 3 a.m. darkness back to the lake.

But this trip was a light workout compared to that Reno trip.

Two cars were available at the lodge. Cobb's 1956 Imperial had no tire chains, but the other car did.

"We'll need both for this operation," he ordered. "One car might get stuck or break down. I'll drive mine and you take the one with chains. You go first. I'll follow your chain marks."

For Cobb to tackle precipitous Route 50 was unthinkable in every way. The Tahoe road, with 200 foot drop-offs, has killed a recorded 80 motorists. Along with his illness, his drunkenness, and no chains, he had bad eyes and was without a driver's license. California had turned him down at his last test; he hadn't bothered to apply in Nevada.

Urging him to ride with me was a waste of breath.

A howling wind hit my car a solid blow as we shoved off. Sleet stuck to the windshield faster than the wipers could work. For the first three miles, snowplows had been active and at 15 mph, in second gear, I managed to hold the road. But then came Spooner's Summit, 7,000 feet high, and then a steep descent of nine miles. Behind me, headlamps blinking, Cobb honked his horn, demanding more speed. Chainless, he wasn't getting traction. *The hell with him,* I thought. Slowing to third gear, fighting to hold a roadbed I couldn't see even with my head stuck out the window, I skidded along. No other traffic moved as we did our crazy tandem around icy curves, at times brushing the guard rails. Cobb was blaring his horn steadily now.

And then here came Cobb.

Tiring of my creeping pace, he gunned the Imperial around me in one big skid. I caught a glimpse of an angry face under a big Stetson hat and a waving fist. He was doing a good 30 mph when he'd gained 25 yards on me, fishtailing right and left, but straightening as he slid out of sight in the thick sleet.

I let him go. Suicide wasn't in my contract.

The next six miles was a matter of feeling my way and praying. Near a curve, I saw tail lights to the left. Pulling up, I found Ty swung sideways and buried, nosedown, in a snow bank, his hind wheels two feet in the air. Twenty yards away was a sheer drop-off into a canyon.

"You hurt?" I asked.

"Bumped my——head," he muttered. He lit a cigar and gave four-letter regards to the Highway Department for not illuminating the "danger" spot. His forehead was bruised and he'd broken his glasses.

In my car, we groped our way down-mountain, a nightmare ride, with Cobb alternately taking in Scotch from a thermos jug and telling me to step on it. At 3 a.m. in Carson City, an all-night garageman used a broom to clean the car of snow and agreed to pick up the Imperial—"when the road's passable." With dawn breaking, we reached Reno. All I wanted was a bed and all Cobb wanted was a craps table.

He was rolling now, pretending he wasn't ill, and with the Scotch bracing him. Ty was able to walk into the Riverside Hotel casino with a hand on my shoulder and without staggering so obviously as usual. Everybody present wanted to meet him. Starlets from a film unit on location in Reno flocked around and comedian Joe E. Lewis had the band play *Sweet Georgia Brown*—Ty's favorite tune.

"Hope your dice are still honest," he told Riverside co-owner Bill Miller. "Last time I was here I won $12,000 in three hours."

"How I remember, Ty," said Miller. "How I remember."

A scientific craps player who'd won and lost huge sums in Nevada in the past, Cobb bet $100 chips, his eyes alert, not missing a play around the board. He soon decided that the table was "cold" and we moved to another casino, then a third. At this last stop, Cobb's legs began to grow shaky. Holding himself up by leaning on the table edge with his forearms, he dropped $300, then had a hot streak in which he won over $800. His voice was a croak as he told the other players, "Watch 'em and weep."

But then suddenly his voice came back. When the stickman raked the dice his way, Cobb loudly said, "You touched the dice with your hand."

"No, sir," said the stickman. "I did *not*."

"I don't lie!" snarled Cobb.

"I don't lie either," insisted the stickman.

"Nobody touches my dice!" Cobb, swaying on his feet, eyes blazing, worked his way around the table toward the croupier. It was a weird tableau. In his crumpled Stetson and expensive camel's-hair coat, stained and charred with cigarette burns, a three-day beard grizzling his face, the gaunt old giant of baseball towered over the dapper gambler.

"You fouled the dice. I saw you," growled Cobb, and then he swung.

The blow missed, as the stickman dodged, but, cursing and almost falling, Cobb seized the wooden rake and smashed it over the table. I jumped in and caught him under the arms as he sagged.

And then, as quickly as possible, we were put into the street by two large uniformed guards. "Sorry, Mr. Cobb," they said, unhappily, "but we can't have this."

A crowd had gathered and as we started down the street, Cobb swearing and stumbling and clinging to me, I couldn't have felt more conspicuous if I'd been strung naked from the neon arch across Reno's main drag, Virginia Street. At the streetcorner, Ty was struck by an attack of breathlessness. "Got to stop," he gasped. Feeling him going limp on me, I turned his six-foot body against a lamppost, braced my legs and with an underarm grip held him there until he caught his breath. He panted and gulped for air.

His face gray, he murmured, "Reach into my left hand coat pocket." Thinking he wanted his bottle of heart pills, I did. But instead pulled out a six-inch-thick wad of currency, secured by a rubber band. "Couple of thousand there," he said weakly. "Don't let it out of sight."

At the nearest motel, where I hired a single, twin-bed room, he collapsed on the bed in his coat and hat and slept. After finding myself some breakfast, I turned in. Hours later I heard him stirring. "What's this place?" he muttered.

I told him the name of the motel—Travelodge.

"Where's the bankroll?"

"In your coat. You're wearing it."

Then he was quiet.

After a night's sleep, Cobb felt well enough to resume his gambling. In the next few days, he won more than $3,000 at the tables, and then we went sightseeing in historic Virginia City. There, as in all places, he stopped traffic. And had the usual altercation. This one was at the Bucket of Blood, where Cobb accused the bartender of serving watered Scotch. The bartender denied it. Crash! Another drink went flying.

Back at the lodge a week later, looking like the wrath of John Barleycorn and having refused medical aid in Reno, he began to suffer new and excruciating pains—in his hips and lower back. But between groans he forced himself to work an hour a day on his autobiography. He told inside baseball tales never published:

". . . Frank Navin, who owned the Detroit club for years, faked his turnstile count to cheat the visiting team and Uncle Sam. So did Big Bill Devery and Frank Farrell, who owned the New York Highlanders—later called the Yankees."

". . . Walter Johnson, the Big Train, tried to kill himself when his wife died."

". . . Grover Cleveland Alexander wasn't drunk out there on the mound, the way people thought—he was an epileptic. Old Pete would fall down with a seizure between innings, then go back and pitch another shutout."

". . . John McGraw hated me because I tweaked his nose in broad daylight in the lobby of the Oriental Hotel, in Dallas, after earlier beating the hell out of his second baseman, Buck Herzog, upstairs in my room."

But before we were well started, Cobb suddenly announced we'd go riding in his 23-foot Chris-Craft speedboat, tied up in a boathouse below the lodge. When I went down to warm it up, I found the boat sunk to the bottom of Lake Tahoe in 15 feet of water.

My host broke all records for blowing his stack when he heard the news. He saw in this a sinister plot. "I told you I've got enemies all around here! It's sabotage as sure as I'm alive!"

A sheriff's investigation turned up no clues. Cobb sat up all night for three nights with his Luger. "I'll salivate the first dirty skunk who steps foot around here after dark," he swore.

Parenthetically, Cobb had a vocabulary all his own. To "salivate" something meant to destroy it. Anything easy was "soft-boiled," to outsmart someone was to "slip him the oskafagus," and all doctors were "truss-fixers." People who displeased him—and this included almost everyone he met—were "fee-simple sonsofbitches," "mugwumps" or (if female) "lousy slits."

Lake Tahoe friends of Cobb's had stopped visiting him long before, but one morning an attractive blonde of about 50 came calling. She was an old chum—in a romantic way, I was given to understand, of bygone years—but Ty greeted her coldly. "Lost my sexual powers when I was 69," he said, when she was out of the room. "What the hell use to me is a woman?"

The lady had brought along a three-section electric vibrator bed, which she claimed would relieve Ty's back pains. We helped him mount it. He took a 20-minute treatment. Attempting to dismount, he lost balance, fell backward, the contraption jackknifed and Cobb was pinned, yelling and swearing, under a pile of machinery.

When I freed him and helped him to a chair, he told the lady—in the choicest gutter language—where she could put her bed. She left, sobbing.

"That's no way to talk to an old friend, Ty," I said. "She was trying to do you a favor."

"And you're a hell of a poor guest around here, too!" he thundered. "You can leave any old time!" He quickly grabbed a bottle and heaved it in my direction.

"Thought you could throw straighter than that!" I yelled back.

Fed up with him, I started to pack my bags. Before I'd finished, Cobb broke out a bottle of vintage Scotch, said I was "damned sensitive," half-apologized, and the matter was forgotten.

While working one morning on an outside observation deck, I heard a thud inside. On his bedroom floor, sprawled on his back, lay Ty. He was unconscious, his eyes rolled back, breathing shallowly. I thought he was dying.

before his strength returned, he was in the usual form.

"They won't let me have a drink," he said, indignantly. "I want you to get me a bottle. Smuggle it in in your tape-recorder case."

I tried, telling myself that no man with terminal cancer deserves to be dried up, but sharp-eyed nurses and orderlies were watching. They searched Ty's closet, found the bottle and over his roars of protest appropriated it.

"We'll have to slip them the oskefagus," said Ty.

Thereafter, a drink of Scotch-and-water sat in plain view in his room, on his bedside table, under the very noses of his physicians—and nobody suspected a thing. The whisky was in an ordinary water glass, and in the liquid reposed Ty's false teeth.

There were no dull moments while Cobb was at the hospital. He was critical of everything. He told one doctor that he was not even qualified to be an interne, and told the hospital dietician—at the top of his voice—that she and the kitchen workers were in a conspiracy to poison him with their "foul" dishes. To a nurse he snapped, "If Florence Nightingale knew about you, she'd spin in her grave."

(Stanford Hospital, incidentally, is one of the largest and top-rated medical plants in the United States.)

But between blasts he did manage to buckle down to work on the book, dictating long into the night into a microphone suspended over his bed. Slowly the stormy details of his professional life came out. He spoke often of having "forgiven" his many baseball enemies, then lashed out at them with such passionate phrases that it was clear he'd done no such thing. High on his "hate" list were McGraw; New York sportswriters; Hub Leonard, a pitcher who in 1926 accused Cobb and Tris Speaker of "fixing" a Detroit-Cleveland game; American League President Ban Johnson; onetime Detroit owner Frank Navin; former Baseball Commissioner Kenesaw Mountain Landis; and all those who intimated that Cobb ever used his spikes on another player without justification.

After a night when he slipped out of the hospital, against all orders, and we drove to a San Francisco Giants-Cincinnati Reds game at Candlestick Park, 30 miles away, Stanford Hospital decided it couldn't help Tyrus R. Cobb, and he was discharged. For extensive treatment his bill ran to more than $1,200.

"That's a nice racket you boys have here," he told the discharging doctors. "You clip the customers and then every time you pass an undertaker, you wink at him."

"Goodbye, Mr. Cobb," snapped the medical men.

Soon after this Ty caught a plane to his native Georgia and I went along. "I want to see some of the old places again before I die," he said.

It now was Christmas eve of 1960 and I'd been with him for three months and completed but four chapters. The project had begun to look hopeless. In Royston, a village of 1,200, Cobb headed for the town cemetery. I drove him there, we parked, and I helped him climb a wind-swept hill through the growing dusk. Light snow fell. Faintly, yule chimes could be heard.

Amongst the many headstones, Ty looked for the plot he'd reserved for himself while in California and couldn't locate it. His temper began to boil. "Dammit, I ordered the biggest damn mausoleum in the graveyard! I know it's around here somewhere." On the next hill, we found it: a large, marble, walk-in-size structure with "Cobb" engraved over the entrance.

"You want to pray with me?" he said, gruffly. We knelt and tears came to his eyes.

Within the tomb, he pointed to crypts occupied by the bodies of his father, Prof. William Herschel Cobb, his mother, Amanda (Chitwood) Cobb, and his sister, Florence, whom he'd had disinterred and placed here. "My father," he said reverently, "was the greatest man I ever knew. He was a scholar, state senator, editor and philosopher. I worshipped him. So did all the people around here. He was the only man who ever made me do his bidding."

Arising painfully, Ty braced himself against the marble crypt that soon would hold his body. There was an eerie silence in the tomb. He said deliberately:

"My father had his head blown off with a shotgun when I was 18 years old—*by a member of my own family*. I didn't get over that. I've never gotten over it."

We went back down the hill to the car. I asked no questions that day.

Later, from family sources and old Georgia friends of the baseball idol, I learned about the killing. One night in August of 1905, they related, Professor Cobb announced that he was driving from Royston to a neighboring village and left home by buggy. But, later that night, he doubled back and crept into his wife's bedroom by way of the window. "He suspected her of being unfaithful to him," said these sources. "He thought he'd catch her in the act. But Amanda Cobb was a good woman. She was all alone when she saw a menacing figure climb through her window and approach her bed. In the dark, she assumed it to be a robber. She kept a shotgun handy by her bed and she used it. Everybody around here knew the story, but it was hushed up when Ty became famous."

News of the killing reached Ty in Augusta, where he was playing minor league ball, on August 9. A few days later he was told that he'd been purchased by the Detroit Tigers, and was to report immediately. "In my grief," Cobb says in the book, "it didn't matter much. . . ."

Came March of 1961 and I remained stuck to the Georgia Peach like court plaster. He'd decided that we were born pals, meant for each other, that we'd complete a baseball book beating anything ever published. He had astonished doctors by rallying from the spreading cancer and, between bouts of transmitting his life and times to a tape-recorder, was raising more whoopee than he had at Lake Tahoe and Reno.

Spring-training time for the big leagues had arrived and we were ensconced in a $30-a-day suite at the Ramada Inn at Scottsdale, Arizona, close by the practice parks of the Red Sox, Indians, Giants and Cubs. Here, each year, Cobb held court. He didn't go to see anybody; Ford Frick, Joe Cronin, Ted Williams, and other diamond notables came to him. While explaining to sportswriters why modern stars couldn't compare to the Wagners, Lajoies, Speakers, Jacksons, Mathewsons and Planks of his day, Ty did other things.

For one, he commissioned a noted Arizona artist to paint him in oils. He was emaciated, having dropped from 208 pounds to 176. The preliminary sketches showed up his sagging cheeks and thin neck.

"I wouldn't let you kalsomine my toilet," ripped out Ty, and fired the artist.

But at analyzing the Dow-Jones averages and playing the stock market, he was anything but eccentric. Twice a week he phoned experts around the country, determined good buys and bought in blocks of 500 to 1,500 shares. He made money consistently, even when bedridden, with a mind that read behind the fluctuations of a dozen different issues. "The State of Georgia," Ty remarked, "will realize about one million dollars from inheritance taxes when I'm dead. But there isn't a man alive who knows what I'm worth." According to the *Sporting News,* there was evidence upon Cobb's death that his worth approximated $12 million. Whatever the true figure, he did not confide the amount to me—or, most probably, to anyone except attorneys who drafted his last will and testament. And Cobb fought off making his will until the last moment.

His fortune began in 1908, when he bought into United (later General) Motors; as of 1961, he was "Mr. Coca Cola," holding more than 20,000 shares of that stock, valued at $85 per share. Wherever we traveled, he carried with him, stuffed into an old brown bag, more than $1 million in stock certificates and negotiable government bonds. The bag never was locked up. Cobb assumed nobody would dare rob him. He tossed the bag into any handy corner of a room, inviting theft. And in Scottsdale it turned up missing.

Playing Sherlock, he narrowed the suspects to a room maid and a man he'd hired to cook meals. When questioned, the maid broke into tears and the cook quit (fired, said Cobb). Hours later, I discovered the bag under a pile of dirty laundry.

Major league owners and league officials hated to see him coming, for he thought their product was putrid and said so, incessantly. "Today they hit for ridiculous averages, can't bunt, can't steal, can't hit-and-run, can't place-hit to the opposite field and you can't call them ballplayers." He told sportswriters, "I blame Frick, Cronin, Bill Harridge, Horace Stoneham, Dan Topping and others for wrecking baseball's traditional league lines. These days, any tax-dodging mugwump with a bankroll can buy a franchise, field some semi-pros and get away with it. Where's our integrity? Where's *baseball?*"

No one could quiet Cobb. Who else had a lifetime average of .367, made

4,191 hits, scored 2,244 runs, won 12 batting titles, stole 892 bases, repeatedly beat whole teams single-handedly? Who was first into the Hall of Fame? Not Babe Ruth—but Cobb, by a landslide vote.

By early April, he could barely make it up the ramp of the Scottsdale Stadium, even hanging onto me. He had to stop, gasping for breath, every few steps. But he kept coming to games—loving the sounds of the ball park. His courage was tremendous. "Always be ready to catch me if I start to fall," he said. "I'd hate to go down in front of the fans."

People of all ages were overcome with emotion upon meeting him; no sports figure I've known produced such an effect upon the public.

We went to buy a cane. At a surgical supply house, Cobb inspected a dozen $25 malacca sticks, bought the cheapest, $4, white-ash cane they had. "I'm a plain man," he informed the clerk, the $7,500 diamond ring on his finger glittering.

But pride kept the old tiger from ever using the cane, any more than he'd wear the $600 hearing aid built into the bow of his glasses.

One day a Mexican taxi-driver aggravated Cobb with his driving. Throwing the fare on the ground, he waited until the cabbie had bent to retrieve it, then tried to punt him like a football.

"What's your sideline," he inquired, "selling opium?"

It was all I could do to keep the driver from swinging on him. Later, a lawyer called on Cobb, threatening a damage suit. "Get in line, there's 500 ahead of you," said Tyrus, waving him away.

Every day was a new adventure. He was fighting back against the pain that engulfed him again—cobalt treatments no longer helped—and I could count on trouble anywhere we went. He threw a salt-shaker at a Phoenix waiter, narrowly missing. One of his most treasured friendships—with Ted Williams—came to an end.

From the early 1940's, Williams had sat at Ty Cobb's feet. They often met, exchanged long letters on the art of batting. At Scottsdale one day, Williams dropped by Ty's rooms. He hugged Ty, fondly rumpled his hair and accepted a drink. Presently the two greatest hitters of past and present fell into an argument over what players should comprise the all-time, all-star team. Williams declared, "I want DiMaggio and Hornsby on my team over anybody you can mention."

Cobb's face grew dark. "Don't give me that! Hornsby couldn't go back for a pop fly and he lacked smartness. DiMaggio couldn't hit with Speaker or Joe Jackson."

"The hell you say!" came back Williams, jauntily. "Hornsby out-hit *you* a couple of years."

Almost leaping from his chair, Cobb shook a fist. He'd been given the insult supreme—for Cobb always resented, and finally hated, Rogers Hornsby. Not until Cobb was in his 16th season did Hornsby top him in the batting averages. "Get . . . away from me!" choked Cobb. "Don't come back!"

Williams left with a quizzical expression, not sure how much Cobb meant it. The old man meant it all the way. He never invited Williams back, nor talked to him, nor spoke his name again. "I cross him off," he told me.

We left Arizona shortly thereafter for my home in Santa Barbara, California. Now failing fast, Tyrus had accepted my invitation to be my guest. Two doctors inspected him at my beach house by the Pacific and gave their opinions: he had a few months of life left, no more. The cancer had invaded the bones of his skull. His pain was intense, unrelenting—requiring heavy sedation—yet with teeth bared and sweat pouring down his face, he fought off medical science. "They'll never get me on their damned hypnotics," he swore. "I'll never die an addict . . . an idiot. . . ."

He shouted, "Where's anybody who cares about me? Where are they? The world's lousy . . . no good."

One night later, on May 1, Cobb sat propped up in bed, overlooking a starlit ocean. He had a habit, each night, of rolling up his trousers and placing them under his pillows—an early-century ballplayer's trick, dating from the time when Ty slept in strange places and might be robbed. I knew that his ever-present Luger was tucked into that pants-roll.

I'd never seen him so sunk in despair. At last the fire was going out. "Do we die a little at a time, or all at once?" he wondered aloud. "I think Max had the right idea."

The reference was to his onetime friend, multimillionaire Max Fleischmann, who'd cheated lingering death by cancer some years earlier by putting a bullet through his brain. Ty spoke of Babe Ruth, another cancer victim. "If Babe had been told what he had in time, he could've got it over with."

Had I left Ty that night, I believe he would have pulled the trigger. His three living children (two were dead) had withdrawn from him. In the wide world that had sung his fame, he had not one intimate friend remaining.

But we talked, and prayed, until dawn, and then sleep came; in the morning, aided by friends, I put him into a car and drove him home, to the big, gloomy house in Atherton. He spoke only twice during the six-hour drive.

"Have you got enough to finish the book?" he asked.

"More than enough."

"Give 'em the word then. I had to fight all my life to survive. They all were against me . . . tried every dirty trick to cut me down. But I beat the bastards and left them in the ditch. Make sure the book says that. . . ."

I was leaving him now, permanently, and I had to ask one question I'd never put to him before.

"Why did you fight so hard in baseball, Ty?"

He'd never looked fiercer than then, when he answered. "I did it for my father, who was an exalted man. They killed him when he was still young. They blew his head off the same week I became a major leaguer. He never got to see me play. But I knew he was watching me and I never let him down."

You can make what you want of that. Keep in mind what Casey Stengel said, later: "I never saw anyone like Cobb. No one even close to him. When he wiggled those wild eyes at a pitcher, you knew you were looking at the one bird nobody could beat. It was like he was superhuman."

To me it seems that the violent death of a father whom a sensitive, highly-talented boy loved deeply, and feared, engendered, through some strangely supreme desire to vindicate that father, the most violent, successful, thoroughly maladjusted personality ever to pass across American sports. The shock tipped the 18-year-old mind, making him capable of incredible feats.

Off the field, he was still at war with the world. For the emotionally disturbed individual, in most cases, does not change his pattern. To reinforce that pattern, he was viciously hazed by Detroit Tiger veterans when he was a rookie. He was bullied, ostracized and beaten up—in one instance, a 210-pound catcher named Charlie Schmidt broke the 165-pound Ty Cobb's nose. It was persecution immediately heaped upon the deepest desolation a young man can experience.

Yes, Ty Cobb was a badly disturbed personality. It is not hard to understand why he spent his entire life in deep conflict. Nor why a member of his family, in the winter of 1960, told me, "I've spent a lot of time terrified of him . . . I think he was psychotic from the time that he left Georgia to play in the big league."

"Psychotic" is not a word I'd care to use. I believe that he was far more than the fiercest of all competitors. He was a vindicator who believed that "father was watching" and who could not put that father's terrible fate out of his mind. The memory of it threatened his sanity.

The fact that he recognized and feared this is revealed in a tape-recording he made, in which he describes his own view of himself: "I was like a steel spring with a growing and dangerous flaw in it. If it is wound too tight or has the slightest weak point, the spring will fly apart and then it is done for. . . ."

The last time I saw him, he was sitting in his armchair in the Atherton mansion. The place still was without lights or heat. I shook his hand in farewell, and he held it a moment longer.

"What about it? Do you think they'll remember me?" He tried to say it as if it didn't matter.

"They'll always remember you," I said.

On July 8, I received in the mail a photograph of Ty's mausoleum on the hillside in the Royston cemetery with the words scribbled on the back: *"Any time now."* Nine days later he died in an Atlanta hospital. Before going, he opened the brown bag, piled $1 million in negotiable securities beside his bed and placed the Luger atop them.

From all of major league baseball, three men and three only appeared for his funeral.

AHAB AND NEMESIS

by A. J. Liebling

This long-time contributor to the New Yorker magazine, one of the most distinguished journalists of the 20th century, died in 1963, eight years after his report of the Moore-Marciano fight.

Back in 1922, the late Heywood Broun, who is not remembered primarily as a boxing writer, wrote a durable account of a combat between the late Benny Leonard and the late Rocky Kansas for the lightweight championship of the world. Leonard was the greatest practitioner of the era, Kansas just a rough, optimistic fellow. In the early rounds, Kansas messed Leonard about, and Broun was profoundly disturbed. A radical in politics, he was a conservative in the arts, and Kansas made him think of Gertrude Stein, *les Six,* and nonrepresentational painting, all of them novelties that irritated him.

"With the opening gong, Rocky Kansas tore into Leonard," he wrote. "He was gauche and inaccurate, but terribly persistent." The classic verities prevailed, however. After a few rounds, during which Broun continued to yearn for a return to a culture with fixed values, he was enabled to record: "The young child of nature who was challenging for the championship dropped his guard, and Leonard hooked a powerful and entirely orthodox blow to the conventional point of the jaw. Down went Rocky Kansas. His past life flashed before him during the nine seconds in which he remained on the floor, and he wished that he had been more faithful as a child in heeding the advice of his boxing teacher. After all, the old masters did know something. There is still a kick in style, and tradition carries a nasty wallop."

I have often thought of Broun's words in the three years since Rocky Marciano, the reigning heavyweight champion, scaled the fistic summits, as they say in *Journal-Americanese,* by beating a sly, powerful quadragenarian colored man named Jersey Joe Walcott. The current Rocky is gauche and inaccurate, but besides being persistent he is a dreadfully severe hitter with either hand. The predominative nature of this asset has been well stated by Pierce Egan, the Edward Gibbon and Sir Thomas Malory of the old London prize ring, who was less preoccupied than Broun with ultimate implications. Writing in 1821 of a "milling cove" named Bill Neat, the Bristol Butcher, Egan said, "He possesses a requisite above all the art that *teaching* can achieve for any boxer; namely, *one hit* from his right hand, given in proper distance, can gain a victory; but three of them are positively enough to dispose of a giant." This is true not only of Marciano's right hand but of his left hand, too—provided he doesn't miss the giant entirely. Egan doubted the advisability of changing Neat's style, and he would have approved of Marciano's. The champion has an apparently unlimited absorptive capacity for percussion (Egan would have called him an "insatiable glutton") and inexhaustible energy ("a prime bottom fighter"). "Shifting," or moving to the side, and "milling in retreat," or moving back, are innovations of the late eighteenth century that Rocky's advisers have carefully kept from his knowledge, lest they spoil his natural prehistoric style. Egan excused these tactics only in boxers of feeble constitution. I imagine Broun would have had a hard time fitting Marciano anywhere into his frame of reference.

Archie Moore, the light-heavyweight champion of the world, who hibernates in San Diego, California, and estivates in Toledo, Ohio, is a Brounian rather than an Eganite in his thinking about style, but he naturally has to do more than think about it. Since the rise of Marciano, Moore, a cerebral and hyper-experienced light-colored pugilist who has been active since 1936, has suffered the pangs of a supreme exponent of *bel canto* who sees himself crowded out of the opera house by a guy who can only shout. As a sequel to a favorable review I wrote of one of his infrequent New York appearances a year ago, when his fee was restricted to a measly five figures, I received a sad little note signed "The most unappreciated fighter in the world, Archie Moore." A fellow who has as much style as Moore tends to overestimate the intellect—he develops the kind of Faustian mind that will throw itself against the problem of perpetual motion, or of how to pick horses first, second, third, *and* fourth in every race. Archie's note made it plain to me that he was honing his harpoon for the White Whale.

When, during some recent peregrinations in Europe, I read newspaper items about Moore's decisioning a large, playful porpoise of a Cuban heavyweight named Nino Valdes and scoop-netting a minnow like Bobo Olson, the middleweight champion, for practice, I thought of him as a lonely Ahab, rehearsing to buck Herman Melville, Pierce Egan, and the betting odds. I did not think that he could bring it off, but I wanted to be there when he tried. What would "Moby Dick" be if Ahab had succeeded? Just another fish story. The thing that is eternally diverting is the struggle of man against history—or what Albert Camus, who used to be an amateur middleweight, has called the Myth of Sisyphus. (Camus would have been a great man to cover the fight, but none of the syndicates thought of it.) When I heard that the boys had been made for September 20th, at the Yankee Stadium, I shortened my stay abroad in order not to miss the Encounter of the Two Heroes, as Egan would have styled the rendezvous.

In London on the night of September 13th, a week before the date set for the Encounter, I tried to get my eye in for fight-watching by attending a bout at the White City greyhound track between Valdes, who had been imported for the occasion, and the British Empire heavyweight champion, Don Cockell, a fat man whose gift for public suffering has enlisted the sympathy of a sentimental people. Since Valdes had gone fifteen rounds with Moore in Las Vegas the previous May, and Cockell had excruciated for nine rounds before being knocked out by Marciano in San Francisco in the same month, the bout offered a dim opportunity for establishing what racing people call a "line" between Moore and Marciano. I didn't get much of an optical workout, because Valdes disposed of Cockell in three rounds. It was evident that Moore and Marciano had not been fighting the same class of people this season.

This was the only fight I ever attended in a steady rainstorm. It had begun in the middle of the afternoon, and while there was a canopy over the ring, the spectators were as wet as speckled trout. "The weather, it is well known, has no terrors to the admirers of Pugilism and Life," Egan once wrote, and on his old stamping ground this still holds true. As I took my seat in a rock pool that had collected in the hollow of my chair, a South African giant named Ewart Potgieter, whose weight had been announced as twenty-two stone ten, was ignoring the doctrine of Apartheid by leaning on a Jamaican colored man who weighed a mere sixteen stone, and by the time I had transposed these statistics to three hundred and eighteen pounds and two hundred and twenty-four pounds, respectively, the exhausted Jamaican had acquiesced in resegregation and retired. The giant had not struck a blow, properly speaking, but had shoved downward a number of times, like a man trying to close an over-filled trunk.

The main bout proved an even less gruelling contest. Valdes, eager to get out of the chill, struck Cockell more vindictively than is his wont, and after a few gestures invocative of commiseration the fat man settled in one corner of the ring as heavily as suet pudding upon the unaccustomed gastric system. He had received what Egan would have called a "ribber" and a "nobber," and when he arose it was seen that the latter had raised a cut on his forehead. At the end of the third round, his manager withdrew him from competition. It was not an inspiring occasion, but after the armistice eight or nine shivering Cubans appeared in the runway behind the press section and jumped up and down to register emotion and restore circulation. *"Ahora Marciano!"* they yelled. "Now for Marciano!" Instead of being grateful for the distraction, the other spectators took a poor view of it. "Sit down, you chaps!" one of them cried. "We want to see the next do!" They were still parked out there in the rain when I tottered into the Shepherd's Bush underground station and collapsed, sneezing, on a train that eventually disgorged me at Oxford Circus, with just enough time left to buy a revivifying draught before eleven o'clock, when the pubs closed. How the mugs I left behind cured themselves I never knew. They had to do it on Bovril.

Because I had engagements that kept me in England until a few days before the Encounter, I had no opportunity to visit the training camps of the rival American Heroes. I knew all the members of both factions, however, and I could imagine what they were thinking. In the plane on the way home, I tried to envision the rival patterns of ratiocination. I could be sure that Marciano, a kind, quiet, imperturbable fellow, would plan to go after Moore and make him fight continuously until he tired enough to become an accessible target. After that, he would expect concussion to accentuate exhaustion and exhaustion to facilitate concussion, until Moore came away from his consciousness, like everybody else Rocky had ever fought. He would try to remember to minimize damage to himself in the beginning, while there was still snap in Moore's arms, because Moore is a sharp puncher. (Like Bill Neat of old, Marciano hits at his opponent's arms when he cannot hit past them. "In one instance, the arm of Oliver [a Neat adversary] received so paralyzing a shock in stopping the blow that it appeared almost useless," Egan once wrote.) Charlie Goldman, Marciano's hand-chipped tactical adviser, would have instructed him in some rudimentary maneuver to throw Moore's first shots off, I felt sure, but after a few minutes Rocky would forget it, or Archie would figure it out. But there would always be Freddie Brown, the "cut man," in the champion's corner to repair superficial damage. One reason Goldman is a great teacher is that he doesn't try to teach a boxer more than he can learn. What he has taught Rocky in the four years since I first saw him fight is to shorten the arc of most of his blows without losing power thereby, and always to follow one hard blow with another—"for insurance"—delivered with the other hand, instead of recoiling to watch the victim fall. The champion has also gained confidence and presence of mind; he has a good fighting head, which is not the same thing as being a good mechanical practitioner. "A *boxer* requires a *nob* as well as a *statesman* does a HEAD, coolness and calculation being essential to *second* his efforts," Egan wrote, and the old historiographer was never more correct. Rocky is thirty-one, not in the first flush of youth for a boxer, but Moore is only a few days short of thirty-nine, so age promised to be in the champion's favor if he kept pressing.

Moore's strategic problem, I reflected on the plane, offered more choices and, as a corollary, infinitely more chances for error. It was possible, but not probable, that jabbing and defensive skill would carry him through fifteen rounds, even on those old legs, but I knew that the mere notion of such a *gambade* would revolt Moore. He is not what Egan would have called a shy fighter. Besides, would Ahab have been content merely to go the distance with the White Whale? I felt sure that Archie planned to knock the champion out, so that he could sign his next batch of letters "The most appreciated and deeply opulent fighter in the world." I surmised that this project would prove a mistake, like Mr. Churchill's attempt to take Gallipoli in 1915, but it would be the kind of mistake that would look good in his memoirs. The basis of what I rightly anticipated would prove a miscalculation went back to Archie's academic background. As a young fighter of conventional tutelage, he must have heard his preceptors say hundreds of times, "They will all go if you hit them right." If a fighter did not believe that, he would be in the position of a Euclidian without faith in the hundred-and-eighty-degree triangle. Moore's strategy, therefore, would be based on working Marciano into a position where he could hit him right. He would not go in and slug with him, because that would be wasteful, distasteful, and injudicious, but he might try to cut him up, in an effort to slow him down so he could hit him right, or else try to

He had honed his harpoon for the White Whale.

hit him right and then cut him up. The puzzle he reserved for me—and Marciano—was the tactic by which he would attempt to attain his strategic objective. In the formation of his views, I believed, Moore would be handicapped, rather than aided, by his active, skeptical mind. One of the odd things about Marciano is that he isn't terribly big. It is hard for a man like Moore, just under six feet tall and weighing about a hundred and eighty pounds, to imagine that a man approximately the same size can be immeasurably stronger than he is. This is particularly true when, like the light-heavyweight champion,

. . . a defeat for the higher faculties

he has spent his whole professional life contending with boxers—some of them considerably bigger—whose strength has proved so near his own that he could move their arms and bodies by cunning pressures. The old classicist would consequently refuse to believe what he was up against.

The light-heavyweight limit is a hundred and seventy-five pounds, and Moore can get down to that when he must, in order to defend his title, but in a heavyweight match each Hero is allowed to weigh whatever he pleases. I was back in time to attend the weighing-in ceremonies, held in the lobby of

. . . but he had made a helluva fight.

Madison Square Garden at noon on the day set for the Encounter, and learned that Moore weighed 188 and Marciano 188¼—a lack of disparity that figured to encourage the rationalist's illusions. I also learned that, in contrast to Jack Solomons, the London promoter who held the Valdes-Cockell match in the rain, the International Boxing Club, which was promoting the Encounter, had decided to postpone it for twenty-four hours, although the weather was clear. The decision was based on apprehension of Hurricane Ione, which, although apparently veering away from New York, might come around again like a lazy left hook and drop in on the point of the Stadium's jaw late in the evening. Nothing like that happened, but the postponement brought the town's theatres and bars another evening of good business from the out-of-town fight trade, such as they always get on the eve of a memorable Encounter. ("Not a bed could be had at any of the villages at an early hour on the preceding evening; and Uxbridge was crowded beyond all former precedent," Egan wrote of the night before Neat beat Oliver.) There was no doubt that the fight had caught the public imagination, ever sensitive to a meeting between Hubris and Nemesis, as the boys on the quarterlies would say, and the bookies were laying 18-5 on Nemesis, according to the boys on the dailies, who always seem to hear. (A friend of mine up from Maryland with a whim and a five-dollar bill couldn't get ten against it in ordinary barroom money anywhere, although he wanted Ahab.)

The enormous—by recent precedent—advance sale of tickets had so elated the I.B.C. that it had decided to replace the usual card of bad preliminary fights with some not worth watching at all, so there was less distraction than usual as we awaited the appearance of the Heroes on the fateful evening. The press seats had been so closely juxtaposed that I could fit in only sidewise between two colleagues—the extra compression having been caused by the injection of a prewar number of movie stars and politicos. The tight quarters were an advantage, in a way, since they facilitated my conversation with Peter Wilson, an English prize-ring correspondent, who happened to be in the row behind me. I had last seen Mr. Wilson at White City the week before, at a time when the water level had already reached his shredded-Latakia mustache. I had feared that he had drowned at ringside, but when I saw him at the Stadium, he assured me that by buttoning the collar of his mackintosh tightly over his nostrils he had been able to make the garment serve as a diving lung, and so survive. Like all British fight writers when they are relieved of the duty of watching British fighters, he was in a holiday mood, and we chatted happily. There is something about the approach of a good fight that renders the spirit insensitive to annoyance; it is only when the amateur of the Sweet Science has some doubts as to how good the main bout will turn out to be that he is avid for the satisfaction to be had from the preliminaries. This is because after the evening is over, he may have only a good supporting fight to remember. There were no such doubts—even in the minds of the mugs who had paid for their

while he is musing about the gate receipts. This had been no lead, and although I certainly hadn't seen Moore throw the punch, I knew that it had landed inside the arc of Marciano's left hook. ("Marciano missed with the right, trun the left, and Moore stepped inside it," my private eye, a trainer named Whitey Bimstein, said next day, confirming my diagnosis, and the film of the fight bore both of us out.) So Ahab had his harpoon in the Whale. He had hit him right if ever I saw a boxer hit right, with a classic brevity and conciseness. Marciano stayed down for two seconds. I do not know what took place in Mr. Moore's breast when he saw him get up. He may have felt, for the moment, like Don Giovanni when the Commendatore's statue grabbed at him—startled because he thought he had killed the guy already—or like Ahab when he saw the Whale take down Fedallah, harpoons and all. Anyway, he hesitated a couple of seconds, and that was reasonable. A man who took nine to come up after a punch like that would be doing well, and the correct tactic would be to go straight in and finish him. But a fellow who came up on two was so strong he would bear investigation.

After that, Moore did go in, but not in a crazy way. He hit Marciano some good, hard, classic shots, and inevitably Marciano, a trader, hit him a few devastating swipes, which slowed him. When the round ended, the edge of Moore's speed was gone, and he knew that he would have to set a new and completely different trap, with diminished resources. After being knocked down, Marciano had stopped throwing that patterned right-and-left combination; he has a good nob. "He never trun it again in the fight," Whitey said next day, but I differ. He threw it in the fifth, and again Moore hit him a peach of a right inside it, but the steam was gone; this time Ahab couldn't even stagger him. Anyway, there was Moore at the end of the second, dragging his shattered faith in the unities and humanities back to his corner. He had hit a guy right, and the guy hadn't gone. But there is no geezer in Moore, any more than there was in the master of the Pequod.

Both came out for the third very gay, as Egan would have said. Marciano had been hit and cut, so he felt acclimated, and Moore was so mad at himself for not having knocked Marciano out that he almost displayed animosity toward him. He may have thought that perhaps he had not hit Marciano *just* right; the true artist is always prone to self-reproach. He would try again. A minute's attention from his squires had raised his spirits and slaked down his hair. At this point, Marciano set about him. He waddled in, hurling his fists with a sublime disregard of probabilities, content to hit an elbow, a biceps, a shoulder, the top of a head—the last supposed to be the least profitable target in the business, since, as every beginner learns, "the head is the hardest part of the human body," and a boxer will only break his hands on it. Many boxers make the systematic presentation of the cranium part of their defensive scheme. The crowd, basically anti-intellectual, screamed encouragement. There was Moore, riding punches, picking them off, slipping them, rolling with them, ducking them, coming gracefully out of his defensive efforts with sharp, patterned blows—and just about holding this parody even on points. His face, emerging at instants from under the storm of arms—his own and Rocky's—looked like that of a swimming walrus. When the round ended, I could see that he was thinking deeply. Marciano came back to his corner at a kind of suppressed dogtrot. He didn't have a worry in the world.

It was in the fourth, though, that I think Sisyphus began to get the idea he couldn't roll back the Rock. Marciano pushed him against the ropes and swung at him for what seemed a full minute without ever landing a punch that a boxer with Moore's background would consider a credit to his workmanship. He kept them coming so fast, though, that Moore tired just getting out of their way. One newspaper account I saw said that at this point Moore "swayed uncertainly," but his motions were about as uncertain as Margot Fonteyn's, or Artur Rubinstein's. He is the most premeditated and best-synchronized swayer in his profession. After the bell rang for the end of the round, the champion hit him a right for good measure—he usually manages to have something on the way all the time—and then pulled back to disclaim any uncouth intention. Moore, no man to be conned, hit him a corker of a punch in return, when he wasn't expecting it. It was a gesture of moral reprobation and also a punch that would give any normal man something to think about between rounds. It was a good thing Moore couldn't see Marciano's face as he came back to his corner, though, because the champion was laughing.

The fifth was a successful round for Moore, and I had him ahead on points that far in the fight. But it took no expert to know where the strength lay. There was even a moment in the round when Moore set himself against the ropes and encouraged Marciano to swing at him, in the hope the champion would swing himself tired. It was a confession that he himself was too tired to do much hitting.

In the sixth, Marciano knocked Moore down twice—once, early in the round, for four seconds, and once, late in the round, for eight seconds, with Moore getting up just before the bell rang. In the seventh, after that near approach to obliteration, the embattled intellect put up its finest stand. Marciano piled out of his corner to finish Moore, and the stylist made him miss so often that it looked, for a fleeting moment, as if the champion were indeed punching himself arm-weary. In fact, Moore began to beat him to the punch. It was Moore's round, certainly, but an old-timer I talked to later averred that one of the body blows Marciano landed in that round was the hardest of the fight.

It was the eighth that ended the competitive phase of the fight. They fought all the way, and in the last third of the round the champion simply overflowed Archie. He knocked him down with a right six seconds before the bell, and I don't think Moore could have got up by ten if the round had lasted that long. The fight by then reminded me of something that Sam Langford, one of the most profound thinkers—and, according to all accounts, one of the greatest doers—of the prize ring, once said to me: "Whatever that other man want to do, don't let him do it." Merely by moving in all the time and punching continually, Marciano achieves the same strategic effect that Langford gained by finesse. It is impossible to think, or to impose your thought, if you have to keep on avoiding punches.

Moore's "game," as old Egan would have called his courage, was beyond reproach. He came out proudly for the ninth, and stood and fought back with all he had, but Marciano slugged him down, and he was counted out with his left arm hooked over the middle rope as he tried to rise. It was a crushing defeat for the higher faculties and a lesson in intellectual humility, but he had made a hell of a fight.

The fight was no sooner over than hundreds of unsavory young yokels with New England accents began a kind of mountain-goat immigration from the bleachers to ringside. They leaped from chair to chair and, after they reached the press section, from typewriter shelf to typewriter shelf and, I hope, from movie star to movie star. "Rocky!" they yelled. "Brockton!" Two of them, as dismal a pair of civic ambassadors as I have seen since I worked on the Providence *Journal & Evening Bulletin,* stood on Wilson's typewriter and yelled "Providence!" After the fighters and the hick delinquents had gone away, I made my way out to Jerome Avenue, where the crowd milled, impenetrable, under the elevated structure. Skirting it as well as I could, I made my way uptown toward 167th Street, the station north of the Stadium.

By boarding a train at 167th Street, you can get a seat before it reaches 161st, which is the Stadium station, and then, if you don't mind people standing on your feet, continue downtown. At least you don't have to fight to get on. If you are not in a great hurry, however (and why should you be at eleven-thirty or twelve on a fight night?), the best plan of all is to walk up to 167th and have a beer in a saloon, or a cup of tea in the 167th Street Cafeteria, and wait until the whole mess clears away. By that time, you may even get a taxi. After this particular fight, I chose the cafeteria, being in a contemplative rather than a convivial mood. The place is of a genre you would expect to find nearer Carnegie Hall, with blond woodwork, and modern functional furniture imported from Italy—an appropriate background for the evaluation of an aesthetic experience. I got my tea and a smoked-salmon sandwich on a soft onion roll at the counter, and made my way to a table, where I found myself between two young policemen who were talking about why Walt Disney has never attempted a screen version of Kafka's "Metamorphosis." As I did not feel qualified to join in that one, I got out my copy of the official program of the fights and began to read the high-class feature articles as I munched my sandwich.

One reminded me that I had seen the first boxing show ever held in Yankee Stadium—on May 12, 1923. I had forgotten that it *was* the first show, and even that 1923 was the year the Stadium opened. In my true youth, the Yankees used to share the Polo Grounds with the Giants, and I had forgotten that, too, because I never cared much about baseball, although, come to think of it, I used to see the Yankees play occasionally in the nineteen-'teens, and should have remembered. I remembered the boxing show itself very well, though. It happened during the spring of my second suspension from college, and I paid five dollars for a high-grandstand seat. The program merely said that it had been "an all-star heavyweight bill promoted by Tex Rickard for the Hearst Milk Fund," but I found that I could still remember every man and every bout on the card. One of the main events was between old Jess Willard, the former heavyweight champion of the world, who had lost the title to Jack Dempsey in 1919, and a young heavyweight named Floyd Johnson. Willard had been coaxed from retirement to make a comeback because there was such a dearth of heavyweight material that Rickard thought he could still get by, but as I remember the old fellow, he couldn't fight a lick. He had a fair left jab and a right uppercut that a fellow had to walk into to get hurt by, and he was big and soft. Johnson was a mauler worse than Rex Layne, and the old man knocked him out. The other main event, *ex aequo,* had Luis Angel Firpo opposing a fellow named Jack McAuliffe II, from Detroit, who had had only fifteen fights and had never beaten anybody, and had a glass jaw. The two winners, of whose identity there was infinitesimal preliminary doubt, were to fight each other for the right to meet the great Jack Dempsey. Firpo was so crude that Marciano would be a Fancy Dan in comparison. He could hit with only one hand—his right—he hadn't the faintest idea of what to do in close, and he never cared much for the business anyway. He knocked McAuliffe out, of course, and then, in a later "elimination" bout, stopped poor old Willard. He subsequently became a legend by going one and a half sensational rounds with Dempsey, in a time that is now represented to us as the golden age of American pugilism.

I reflected with satisfaction that old Ahab Moore could have whipped all four principals on that card within fifteen rounds, and that while Dempsey may have been a great champion, he had less to beat than Marciano. I felt the satisfaction because it proved that the world isn't going backward, if you can just stay young enough to remember what it was really like when you were really young.

PEANUT VENDOR

by Quentin Reynolds

How an American gastronomical institution got its start more than thirty years ago.

Harry Stevens stood there in the back of the grandstand and looked very, very unhappy. Usually a crowd of fifty thousand fans at a ball game was reason enough to make Harry beam, but today the crowd brought no smile to the Stevens face, because of the weather. It was so cold that the Giant infielders going through their pre-game practice were trying vainly to get the numbness out of their hands and the crowd sat huddled miserably with coat collars turned up.

The game really should have been called off, but baseball magnates hate to disappoint a crowd of fifty thousand—especially when those fifty thousand have already laid their dough on the line and bought tickets. At that time Harry Stevens was a purveyor of score-cards, ice cream and soda pop. The crowd had bought the score-cards all right, but who would buy ice cream and ice-cold soda on a day like this? Harry had stocked up heavily with ice cream, anticipating a warm day, and ice cream doesn't keep forever.

Harry Stevens stood there for a moment thinking very, very fast and when he got down to thinking fast he could think very fast indeed. He was a salesman. Here was a crowd. Somehow the two had to get together. Then . . .

"Hey, you," Stevens called to one of his men. "Get the boys up here. Hurry up. I've got an idea."

He had an idea that was going to make him five million dollars within the next few years—though he didn't know it at the time. His son Frank had bobbed up with it only a few days before, but then he hadn't thought much of it. Now was a good time to try it out.

"Send around to all the butchers in the neighborhood," Stevens barked at his assistant. "Buy up all of those German sausages you can, those long dachshund sausages—what do they call 'em, frankfurters? Then hustle around to the bakers in the neighborhood and buy up all the rolls you can find. These people want something hot. We'll give them something hot. And get some mustard. Yes, mustard—and hurry up."

"The boss has gone nuts," his men grumbled, but they hustled out to the butchers and they came back with yards of the "dachshund" sausages Stevens had ordered.

They had a small kitchen under the stands and under Harry's direction they heated the frankfurters and then Harry himself smeared them with mustard (later the mustard became optional) and stuck them between the sliced halves of the rolls.

"Take 'em out and sell 'em," Harry barked to his astonished men. "Call out that they're 'red-hot.' Remember that, 'red-hot.' Those people are freezing. They'll want something hot."

"Red-hot," the boys called as they went up and down the aisles. "Get a red-hot dachshund sausage in a roll. Dachshund sandwiches . . . red-hot . . ."

The crowd bought them through curiosity at first—then with enthusiasm. The incomparable Tad, greatest of newspaper sports cartoonists and phrase-maker extraordinary, was sitting in the press box watching the game. Always on the alert for something new, he watched the crowd devouring the new delicacy.

"Dachshund—that means dog. Why not call them hot dogs?" Tad mused, and not long after, in a cartoon, he immortalized the frankfurter which Stevens had naturalized, under the name of "hot dog." The implication that stray mongrel dogs sneaking optimistically into butcher shops to wangle a bit of free beef came out in the form of frankfurters, or "hot dogs," did not detract from the tremendous popularity of the German-born tidbit. This was in the early part of the century and ever since then hot dogs have been an integral adjunct of ball games, race tracks, six-day bike events and fights. That cold day which had begun so dolefully really made the Stevens' fortune and helped considerably in making Harry M. Stevens, Incorporated, the largest firm of outdoor caterers in the world.

Harry Stevens died about two years ago. A personality while he lived, he is on his way to becoming a legend. There is seldom anything as dull as the story of a self-made man who went on to become wealthy, but there is nothing dull about the story of Harry Stevens, and besides, Stevens really isn't dead at all.

His three sons now run the business he founded and they run it exactly as he did and when they get into difficulties they get together and say, "What would Father have done in a situation like this?" And they figure out what he would have done and they do it—so you really can't say that Harry Stevens is dead.

No brothers were ever closer than Hal, Joe and Frank Stevens, and perhaps it's because old Harry left a bit of his spirit to each so that each is necessary to the others and the three together are a composite mind which was once Harry Stevens. And they talk of Harry Stevens not as sons usually do of fathers—not sadly or in a reminiscent vein, but cheerfully and proudly, as though he still lived; and I tell you when you hear them talking of him in their New York offices, or at Hialeah, or at the Polo Grounds, or at Saratoga, or at Madison Square Garden, you feel that old Harry is very, very much alive. Well, anyhow here's the story of Harry Stevens, the story which within a few years will be a legend.

When Harry Stevens was twenty-one he took a look around his native London and decided that it was too crowded with old men. A young man had to wait until an old man died before he could get a chance to show his wares and, even at twenty-one, Harry felt that he had something. If nothing else he had a questioning mind—but he couldn't find the answers in London. So he married and brought his bride to that land called America for her honeymoon. He landed in New York with five dollars and a high heart. The five dollars didn't last long, but the high heart did.

He worked at odd jobs around New York for a while, but they were hard dollars he was making. Someone told him about a steel mill at a place called Niles where there were plenty of jobs—steady jobs too, at good salaries. He didn't quite know where Niles was, but that didn't matter. He and his bride saved and scrimped and soon had raised the necessary get-away money. When he went to the ticket office to ask for two tickets to Niles the ticket seller asked, "What Niles? Niles, Michigan, or Niles, Ohio?"

"It's the place that has a steel mill," Harry suggested helpfully.

"Well," the ticket agent said doubtfully, "I never heard of no steel mills at Niles, Michigan, so maybe it's Niles, Ohio, you're looking for."

His guess was right, and lucky it was for both Harry and for Niles, Ohio, for many years afterwards Niles became the recipient of some of his charities. For a few years Harry worked in Niles as a steel puddler. It was good, steady work and if occasionally Harry saw visions and had restless dreams which told him that he was capable of conquering greater worlds he brushed such aside, for he had children now, and responsibilities, and he couldn't afford to fool around with those wildcat schemes that sometimes took possession of his mind.

One day Harry found himself with an idle afternoon, and destiny led his footsteps into the Columbus baseball park. It must have been destiny because Harry had never seen a baseball game and had no interest in seeing one. Something just led his steps into that ball park. He bought a score-card, hoping to be enlightened as to just what this rather silly-looking performance was all about, but the score-card was only a printed slip of paper with the names of the players on it. There were no advertisements and it developed that the line-up as printed was hopelessly inaccurate.

Stevens sat there looking at the score-card and something began to stir in his consciousness. Perhaps you'd call it the instinct of the born salesman, or of the born showman, for Harry was always both.

"This score-card is ridiculous," Harry told himself. "It could be improved. It could be made to make money. It could . . ."

He arose and went to the office of the owner of the club. He said he'd like to handle the score-card concession for the Columbus ball park on a fifty-fifty basis. The owner said he'd sell the concession for the season outright for five hundred dollars. Stevens airily agreed to the terms (he didn't have three dollars in his pocket) and left the office.

He found a printer who would work, for a short time, on credit. He went to every merchant in Columbus, soliciting advertisements, and the next day he turned up at the ball park with seven hundred dollars, the proceeds of this super-salesmanship. He gave the owner of the club his five hundred dollars and proceeded to print and sell the score-cards.

Stevens was one of the greatest practical psychologists of his time. I suppose any great salesman is a great psychologist. Stevens was right so often and wrong so seldom that he must have had an instinct for salesmanship, and for understanding the wants of crowds, that transcended mere brilliancy. Until he began selling his score-cards no one really thought it necessary to have one. He educated the fans to the point where they felt that they couldn't enjoy the game without one of his cards. And he did it with a sentence.

. . . the friend of millionaires, of sportsmen. (With Col. Ruppert, 1917.)

"Dachshund—that means dog. Why not call them hot dogs?"

"You can't tell the players without a score-card," he'd cry as he stood before the entrance of the ball park while the crowd poured in. They couldn't miss him. He wore a bright red coat, a tall, battered hat and his voice was booming Jovian thunder that couldn't be ignored.

Harry was on his way now, but he didn't make enough to do much for his family, which had been increased by another son. He branched out and got the score-card concession at Toledo and Milwaukee and he exhibited a fine stroke of genius by printing the Milwaukee score-cards in German.

Then he took a great stride forward. He tackled the big-league parks. First it was Pittsburgh, then Boston and then Washington, and he was known as the Score-Card King. There wasn't much profit in score-cards, though, and a couple of rained-out games would set him back two or three weeks' profit.

He still maintained his method of personal salesmanship. At Washington, for instance, he'd announce important personages as they entered the park.

"Here's Senator Smith coming in now," his voice would boom. "Of course the senator is going to buy a program. He knows you can't tell the players without a program. And here's Senator Jones. Here's your box, Senator. Let me brush off that chair. And of course you want a program; you can't . . ."

Harry Stevens became a character with his red coat and his battered hat. People would point at him as he went up and down the aisles and they'd say, "That's Harry Stevens." They'd enjoy his patter whether they bought or not.

Vaguely Stevens realized that there were great possibilities which he hadn't as yet touched in this business of being a concessionaire. Where would he find the biggest opportunities? New York, of course. At that time—this was in the early 1890's—New York was the goal of every young man. Harry decided that he'd have to conquer New York next.

He met John Montgomery Ward at the Pittsburgh ball park one day. Ward was then manager of the New York Giants.

"I'd like to sell score-cards in your ball park," he told Ward.

"Sure—why not?" Ward replied. "I like to hear you sell 'em."

Stevens liquidated his assets, found that the results would pay his fare to New York and allow him to live for a week or two, and then he headed for Bagdad-on-the-Hudson. The New York of the nineties—loud, blustering, rowdy, vital—was just suited to Stevens. He could speak the language of New York. And he could out-shout New York.

He became a fixture at the entrance to the Polo Grounds. He introduced a new bit of patter. The Giants would be playing Pittsburgh. Late-comers, hurrying into the park, would be stopped by Harry.

"Pittsburgh is leading 3 to 2," he'd cry. "George Gore is at bat and Danny Richardson on first . . . Here you are . . . you can't tell the players without a program."

He was doing all right but only all right, for these were lean years for the Giants. In 1901 the Giants finished last in the then twelve-team league. Then in the middle of the 1902 season there came a scrappy little man named John McGraw to manage the club. In 1903 he got the team up to a point where it finished in second place. New York began to take an interest in the team—and come to the games. This all helped Stevens and he put in a sideline of ice cream and soda pop. In 1904 McGraw won the pennant—and the Giants became a New York institution. Fans stormed the ball park and there was Harry in his red coat waiting for them. He had to hire assistants but he kept on hawking score-cards himself. Why, he sold twice as many as the best man he ever hired.

He added peanuts to his stock and a few years later he was to be known as the man who parlayed a peanut into a million dollars. One thing worried him a bit these days. He wasn't selling much soda pop. He reasoned that the peanuts should make the customers thirsty—but still he didn't sell much pop. Then he realized why.

Baseball fans are like no other fans on earth. They come to a game and, by golly, they want to see the game; they want to see every moment of it. They can't take their eyes off that diamond. Not long enough even to tilt a bottle of soda up to their lips. When you drink soda out of a bottle you have to bend your head back, and thus, for a second, take your eyes from the diamond. Stevens reasoned that out—and found the answer.

He discovered the straw. He put two straws into each bottle and the fans could drink all they wanted without missing anything. There weren't many angles that Stevens didn't know—very few corners he couldn't turn.

About this time Harry fell in love. He fell in love with the Giants. He became the greatest fan the Giants ever had. Perhaps he knew that he was on his way to a fortune and in the beginning felt that McGraw's success with the Giants had brought in the crowds that were making him rich. But finally he became just a dyed-in-the-wool, eighteen-karat Giant fan. Once after the Giants lost a tough one a friend saw Harry looking very sad.

"A tough one to blow, Harry," he said.

Stevens turned to Addison for solace:

" 'Tis not in mortals to command success,
But we'll do more, Sempronius. We'll deserve it."

Often there were rumors that he was about to buy the Giants. He'd snort angrily when this was mentioned to him.

"What?" he'd storm. "Me buy a ball club? Say, I'm a fan, a real fan. To me baseball is a sport, a hobby. I couldn't turn a hobby into a business."

Now he was reaching out, grabbing the concession at this ball park, at that one; at this race track and that. Six-day bike races were popular then and he got the concession at the old Madison Square Garden. He opened the roof there, too. One night he was talking to one of the diners at the roof, an architect named Stanford White. Near by a man was pacing nervously up and down waiting for Harry to finish talking to White. Harry finally said good night and turned his back. The nervous man came up and put a bullet through White. The nervous man was Harry Thaw.

Stevens grew in stature and became the friend of millionaires, of sportsmen —of New Yorkers. He got the concession at the Saratoga race track through the good offices of William C. Whitney, former Secretary of State, the father of Harry Payne Whitney and the founder of the Whitney financial dynasty. One day at Saratoga he met Whitney.

"How much money can you raise immediately?" Whitney asked him gruffly.

"I don't know, maybe thirty or thirty-five thousand dollars," Stevens answered, perplexed.

"Get it and give it to me," Whitney said—and Stevens for once stilled his questioning mind and handed the money over to Whitney.

Not long afterwards Whitney handed him a check for $215,000—the profits of a stock-market transaction he had put Harry in. Now Harry was wealthy and his sons were grown and they took part of the burden off his shoulders. But wealth to him was only a means of expanding. He took on the Juarez race track and adopted the slogan, "From the Hudson to the Rio Grande." It's still on the letterhead of the firm. August Belmont built his beautiful Belmont Park on Long Island. He came to Stevens and said, "Name your terms, Harry, you've got to set this table."

He was older now and if you didn't know him you might have thought he was a cranky sort of person but, as Damon Runyon once said of him, "He's a great guy to have in your corner when you're fighting Old Man Trouble."

He never lost interest in the active management of the business. You'd see him there at the Polo Grounds watching the conduct of his venders. Westbrook Pegler, that writer of acid paragraphs, tells a story of the rage shown by the old man when he'd catch a kid who was supposed to be selling peanuts taking time out to watch the ball game.

"Harry's eye would light on some kid who was sitting down in the aisle," Pegler says, "and Harry would roar, 'Hey! Hey! Hey!' scaring the kid half to death. But if one of those kids didn't show up for work and the old man found out that it was because the kid was sick, why, he'd send his car around with a basket of food and a fifty-dollar bill. Then you'd never hear him yell, 'Hey! Hey! Hey!' at all. Instead, he'd be so quiet no one but the kid and he ever knew about it."

Two years ago, Stevens, having lived a full life, died. But he left an impressive monument. He left a business which is just as successful today as it was when he died. And his sons, Hal and Joe and Frank (and Frank's son, Harry, second) will tell you that they head the most successful catering concern in the world because they run it exactly as their father ran it and they'll continue to run it that way.

Go behind the scenes at a ball park and you'll see the printing presses which print the score-cards and the hot bins for the peanuts and the cold storage for the ice cream and the huge sterilized cans where the hot dogs are kept—you'll see them but they are only the physical manifestations of a business which sometimes caters to as many as 300,000 people a day. You won't see the spirit of Harry Stevens, the man who made an American citizen out of the frankfurter, who made the peanut an institution, and who died without having ever had any man say of him, "He cheated me."

THE GREATEST MAN

by Red Smith

The dean of American sports writers, who twice won the
Grantland Rice Memorial Award for excellence in his field,
paid tribute to a lovable, triple-talking curmudgeon in 1965.

Mrs. Charles Shipman Payson, who owns the New York Mets, spoke with simple sincerity. "He is the greatest man I ever met in baseball," she said. "He is the greatest man I ever met." She dabbed at a tear. So did Mrs. Edna Stengel.

This was in the Colonnade Room off the lobby of the Essex House where Charles Dillon Stengel limped to the end of a journey he began 55 years ago in Kankakee, Ill. Well, not exactly the end. Though Casey Stengel announced his retirement as manager of the Mets yesterday, he's too young to quit baseball altogether.

In his 76th year he will serve the team as vice-president in charge of West Coast operations, meaning that he'll operate from his home in Glendale, Calif., employing his fame and personality and persuasive eloquence to influence boys who can run fast and throw hard.

"I'm probably going to be the highest priced scout you ever heard of," he told the press.

He looked across at Mrs. Stengel, who was toying with a replica of the steel ball in her husband's broken hip.

"She's gonna like it," Casey said, "I guess."

The announcement was not unexpected, for when Casey had the fall that put him in a hospital a few weeks ago, everybody realized that the injury could mean no more activity for him in the dugout and on the field. Yet when it came it seemed sudden. It is not easy to imagine the baseball scene without that gnarled figure in the middle of it.

The Mets fielded their first team for the occasion—Don Grant, chairman of the board, Mrs. Payson, Casey, Edna, George Weiss, president, and Wes Westrum, the interim manager who will continue in that capacity for the rest of the season at least.

Casey arrived leaning on a metal cane. His face looked drawn at first, perhaps reflecting the boredom of his convalescence in the Essex House where his audiences are smaller than those he is accustomed to. After he'd been talking for a while—about baseball and the astronauts Cooper and Conrad and the young

—an authentic original.